Pat Chapman's *Favourite*
MIDDLE
EASTERN
R E C I P E S

Pat Chapman's *Favourite*

MIDDLE EASTERN

RECIPES

PIATKUS

© 1989 Pat Chapman

First published as *Curry Club Favourite
Middle Eastern Recipes* in 1989 by
Judy Piatkus (Publishers) Limited
5 Windmill Street, London W1

First paperback edition 1992

This revised paperback edition first published in 1996

ISBN 0–7499–1540–4 (Pbk)

Edited by Susan Fleming
Design by Paul Saunders
Illustrated by Zena Flax and Hanife Hassan
Map on pages 16 and 17 by Dick Vine
Photography by Tim Imrie

The publishers would like to thank Cloudfair Ltd, London NW10
for the loan of copper items used in the photographs,
and Fergule Ozguven for the loan of her hand-painted tiles

Cover photograph shows Chicken with Dates and Honey (page 101)
and Stir-Fried Okra (pages 125–6)

Phototypeset in 11/12pt Lasercomp Sabon
Printed and bound in Great Britain by
Butler & Tanner Ltd, Frome and London

CONTENTS

INTRODUCTION

MIDDLE Eastern cuisine has its roots at the beginning of civilization, thousands of years ago. Bread-making, brewing, wine-making, yoghurt, kebabs and probably cooking itself originated there, yet I suspect that a great many of us born and living in the 'West' know relatively little about the food of the Middle East. Its image is sometimes fanciful and off-putting – of arid deserts and scarcity of water, of millennia of careful 'waste-not-want-not' attitudes which meant the eating of sheep's eyes, and lizards', locusts' and camels' testicles, hooves, tails and tongues. These may be luxuries to Bedouin tribes, and I certainly have recipes in my personal collection for such items, but it is not the normal everyday fare enjoyed by the masses. Their food is wholesome, varied and delicious. Nutritionally it makes best use of the enormous range of produce in the area: fresh fruit and vegetables, meat, poultry and fish, nuts, grain and dairy produce, spices and herbs. All these are to hand and they are prepared in innumerable and delicious ways.

Yet, despite the plethora of 'ethnic' restaurants in the UK, notably Indo-Pakistani and Chinese, there are relatively few dedicated to Middle Eastern food, particularly outside London. The most prolific are probably Greek, Turkish and Cypriot. Most UK cities boast at least one or two of these. Next come Lebanese, then Persian and Moroccan, and there are even fewer Armenian. Some countries are not represented at all. In total there are about 200 such restaurants in the UK, and nearly all of those follow a very well-worn 'formula' menu of 'safe-bet' favourites. You'd be forgiven for believing that Middle Eastern food consists only of houmous, taramasalata, doner kebabs, shish kebabs, roast meat or poultry, rice, pitta bread, yoghurt, fruity desserts, thick coffee and Turkish Delight. All these items do exist, of course. I love them all, and recipes for them appear in this book. They have their rightful place in the Middle Eastern repertoire, but, as you might suspect, they are only the tip of an enormous edible Middle Eastern iceberg of culinary delights.

But what is meant by the term the 'Middle East'? Technically there are 14 countries defined on the map on pages 16 and 17: Syria, Lebanon, Jordan,

Iraq, Iran, Egypt, Saudi Arabia, the United Arab Emirates, and six further Gulf states. They have in common the Arabic tongue, thousands of years of history and culture, the Islamic religion, and their cuisine. When I first started to think about writing a Middle Eastern cookbook, years ago, I literally thought that I would confine myself to these fourteen countries.

However, as any visitor to the North African Mediterranean countries knows, the people there have an Arabic way of life, with a cuisine which, whilst it has a lot in common with its Middle Eastern neighbours, has a lot of dishes and cooking methods which are unique to the area, Moroccan food in particular being absolutely superb. So as far as this book is concerned, the four Maghreb countries of Morocco, Algeria, Tunisia and Libya have also been included.

Then to the immediate north of the Middle East lies Turkey. It straddles Europe and Asia, has its own language and culture, and whilst not a part of the recognized Middle East, it has always had deep roots in the Arab-Islamic world and vice versa. Turkish food was developed very largely by its extravagant Ottoman Emperors, and whilst it is distinctively different from that of the Middle East, it has had a great influence on it, and again I could not omit it from this book. At its height, the Ottoman Empire ruled Greece and Cyprus. Again, culinary ideas cross-fertilized between these three countries, so I have included a few Greek recipes and a Cypriot recipe.

There are three other places, each once a kingdom in its own right, which over the millennia have played their part in shaping the Middle East. Today they are known as Armenia, Azerbaijan and Georgia, and they are now republics of the USSR. Their cooking cannot be ignored in Middle Eastern terms, and I have included a number of their recipes.

Finally, in the middle of the 'Middle East' is Israel, whose food is fundamentally Arabic, but which has benefited from the innovations and traditions of its new immigrants over the last four decades.

So there we have it: a total of twenty-five countries in three continents, Africa, Europe and Asia; 227 million people speaking many languages and of several creeds; people with fundamental differences, but with much in common. And perhaps the greatest thing they have in common is their food.

Over the years I have visited a good many of these twenty-five countries. I have been able to amass a huge collection of information and recipes. I have also included a considerable amount of supplementary information about Middle Eastern food and culture. And, although this book concentrates largely on traditional Middle Eastern cooking, with many of the recipes originating in antiquity, I must make the point that every single dish is a contemporary dish, eaten and relished by today's 'Middle Eastern' people. However, I make no apology for omitting the latest plasto-putty contributions to the Middle Eastern street-side scene such as the 'san-weech', the 'Veempee', the 'Qentuqi Cheekeen', 'makaronee', the 'peezah',

'Coki-Peps' and 'Wreeglees'. Endearing though these translations are it is sad that big business has penetrated the ancient world. Although these mass-produced manifestations are gaining a hold, particularly with younger city dwellers, I doubt that they will ever supersede the culinary wonders which have evolved, over thousands of years, into the truly outstanding dishes of the Middle East.

Pat Chapman
The Curry Club, Haslemere, Surrey

CHAPTER 1

CULINARY BACKGROUND

BEFORE we get down to the business of the recipes, I'd like to give you an insight into the lands which are the culinary Middle East. There are twenty-five countries grouped together for the purpose of this book; some are at war with their neighbours, and have little in common but hatred; others are thousands of miles apart physically but are close politically. Some are in Russia, some in Europe, some in Africa and most are in Asia. Each has a fascinating past which goes back to the beginnings of civilization itself, and it is their common history and ancestry which provides their culinary links.

So join me on a journey over 12,000 years and 10,000 miles as we meet the 230 million people of the Middle East, their twenty-five countries, and above all their wonderful food.

THE MAGHREB: MOROCCO, ALGERIA, TUNISIA AND LIBYA

Many of us are first introduced to the Arabic way of life by means of a holiday in Morocco or Tunisia. Those that venture out of their package cocoon and into the ancient towns find that little has changed over the centuries, and to many, this comes as a culture shock. They see a largely peasant population whose language, religion and very existence owe most to the influence of 1,000 years of Arab rule.

Centuries ago, Morocco, Algeria and Tunisia were one country known as the Maghreb – 'the land of the setting sun' or 'the land at the end of the world', for in those days the Atlantic ocean was the edge of a flat world beyond which it was believed that injudicious mariners would fall off. The original inhabitants of the area were the nomadic, primitive Berbers. Still nomadic, fierce, pale-skinned and blue-eyed, the Berbers are to be found in Morocco, and are easily distinguished by their long brown and white robes with peaked hoods.

From about AD 700, a succession of Arabs ruled the Maghreb, bringing in their culture and Islam. Little changed when power shifted to the Turkish Ottoman Empire in 1535. By 1715 the Ottomans had relinquished control, and Libya, under the name of Tripoli, was created at that time. The departure of the Ottomans eventually allowed European colonizers to move in, and Spain, France and Italy took possession of the various lands of the Maghreb.

Independence came to Libya in 1951, Tunisia and Morocco in 1956, Algeria in 1962.

The cooking of the four Maghreb countries has strong Arab and Ottoman roots, even a Persian influence, yet it has a unique style, resulting from the continuous presence of the Berbers. Other influences have come from invaders such as the Carthaginians, who used the Maghreb coasts for trading posts and bases in the centuries before Christ, and who probably introduced durum wheat flour and the process of making semolina. From this decidedly Italian food, the Berbers invented the Maghreb's most celebrated dish: couscous. It consists of small grains of semolina which are steamed to tenderness over a pot of meat, poultry or vegetable broth.

Of the four Maghrebi countries Libyan cooking perhaps shows the most obvious Arab influence. It has also been influenced by Italy, but 'haute cuisine' does not play a large part in contemporary Libya, where, despite the discovery of oil, poverty is prevalent. Nevertheless, Libya has some excellent dishes which I have included in this book (see pages 58, 64, 113 and 151).

Tunisian food has had a very obvious Italian influence, with pasta and tomatoes making frequent appearances. They also adore extremely hot food. Their red chilli paste, harissa, appears on the table at every meal time including breakfast.

Algeria has been very strongly influenced recently by France and it uses little spice in its cooking. The Algerian *chakchouka* (ratatouille) should not be missed.

It is Moroccan cooking which stands out as one of the best, not only of the Maghreb, but of the whole Middle East. It is complex and varied, delicious and full of surprises. It has taken the best of the Arab and Turkish repertoires, added a uniqueness of its own, and undoubtedly gained from the more recent French influences. Moroccan cooking uses spices effectively, and in some cases liberally. It uses the world's most extraordinary spice mixture, *ras-el-hanout*, in some dishes, yet in others a single spice (cummin is very popular) is all that is called for. The spicy paste *chermoula* is a particularly popular marinade, used with fish, meat and poultry which is then spit roasted, sometimes stuffed, or is glazed with spices, nuts and honey.

Moroccan dishes require a special pastry called *warkha*, which requires years of practice and skill to make, and I have stood for hours watching it being done in a Tangiers bakery. The best *warkha* should be thinner than tracing paper. *Briouats* (called *breiks* in Tunisia and *bourek* in Algeria) are small pastries made from *warkha* with various fillings. But the *warkha* which is often regarded as Morocco's real masterpiece is *bisteeya*, a pie containing ground pigeon, nuts, dried fruit, scrambled eggs and spices, and seasoned finally with sugar and lemon juice. This intriguing mixture of savoury, sweet and sour, so typically Persian in origin, appears elsewhere in the Maghreb. But I must allow myself the memory of drooling on many occasions at the Moroccan baker trying to decide whether to invest in *m'hancha* – the snake cake made from *warkha* pastry stuffed with almond paste, rolled into a tight sausage, coiled into a Catherine wheel, baked then sprinkled with icing sugar and a lattice of ground cinnamon – or perhaps a *shebbakia*, curly pastry ribbons, deep-fried then soaked in honey and spinkled with sesame seeds, or indeed a dozen other astonishing pastry delights. The choice was not made easier whilst sipping that great Moroccan experience, mint tea or *naa'naa*.

EGYPT

Of all the countries of the Middle East, none has a more colourful past than Egypt. The original inhabitants, the Hammites, had moved into Egypt by 4500 BC. There they took advantage of the highly fertile delta of the river Nile, the world's longest river, to establish a civilization. By 2900 BC the world's first kingdom was established, and the Pharaohs were to rule virtually uninterrupted for nearly 3,000 years, an achievement unequalled by any other civilization. The Pharaohs eventually succumbed to Rome in 30 BC, then Egypt fell to the Moslem Arabs by 642. It remained under a succession of Caliphates and Sultanates for nearly 900 years until taken over by the Ottoman Turks in 1517. Ottoman power began to fail in the late nineteenth century. Napoleon Bonaparte imposed French influence there in 1798, resulting in the opening of the French-conceived Suez Canal in 1869. Egypt achieved independence in 1947. Although the greater part of the Egyptian population is now Moslem, there is a strong Christian community, the Copts, who are the direct descendants of the Pharaohic Egyptians, and many Egyptian dishes have descended virtually unaltered from those times.

The Egyptians adore certain spices, such as cummin (of which they are a world-class exporter) and garlicky tastes, typified in *ta'leya*. They do not relish chilli heat. Bean and pulse dishes are popular such as *ful medamis, ful nabed*, and *ads bi gibba*. Egyptians are also prolific egg eaters, and in Pharaohic days they operated egg hatcheries with incubators. *Eggahs* and *tzazegh* are delicious omelettes. Poultry is equally popular, as well as *kibda ma'liya* (goose liver), *siman bil kibbeh* (quail) and *firri bil fireek* (pigeon). Unusual vegetables include *melokhia* and *fattoush*, often eaten with *aish* (bread), and one of Egypt's most famous dishes is felafel (croquettes), which is popular all over the Middle East.

ISRAEL

Currently, Israel has a population of 3.5 million. Few of those were native to the area, the remainder were Jews in 'exile' in Western countries who returned to Israel after its formation in 1948, bringing a 'modern' outlook and technology to a very barren land. Irrigation and agriculture have produced fertile farm lands on which grow superb quality vegetables and fruit. Adroit marketing has made the Israeli orange, capsicum, avocado, melon, okra and courgettes readily available throughout Europe. Geese are also reared in quantity for export to France, specifically for pâté de foie gras. And there is substantial beef, dairy, poultry and egg production.

Many Israeli dishes are familiar all over the world wherever there are Jewish communities. Their origins are lost to history, but they certainly owe much to the traditional cooking styles of the Middle East. Some dishes are similar, if not identical, to those of neighbouring countries. The felafel, for example, is regarded as an Israeli national dish.

The strict rules of kosher cooking have resulted in some well-known and superb dishes unique to Israel. Latkes, for example, are pancakes made from grated potato and onion dipped in batter and fried. Jews may not cook on the Sabbath and *cholent*, a spiced stew of meat and vegetables, is started the evening before so that it is still hot at lunchtime. *Gefilte* are fish balls, and the bagel the well-known bread. One very modern dish from Israel is *sabra* dip, made from avocados. Israeli desserts include *blintze*, a sweet pancake with curd cheese, and *sephardi*, stuffed dates.

THE LEVANT: JORDAN, PALESTINE, LEBANON, SYRIA AND IRAQ

It was in the hugely fertile crescent created by the rivers Euphrates and Tigris that man first became civilized. Some 12,000 years ago he learned to farm, to domesticate himself and his animals, to build cities and to trade. Later the area became 'the granary' of the Roman Empire. The Arabs took possession from AD 700 to the fifteenth century, during which time many Arab cities were developed to exploit their spice trade with Europe. The decline of the Arab spice monopoly brought about a vacuum which the Turkish Ottomans were soon to fill. The end of World War I saw the dismantling of that empire and the formation of Jordan, Palestine, Lebanon, Syria and Iraq as independent states.

Before its present troubles, and unlike its neighbours, Lebanon had a highly sophisticated restaurant tradition instigated by its French colonists. Beirut was a fashionable tourist resort of great beauty, and I well remember its curving bay, twinkling lights, yachts and sunsets, its wealth and its restaurants. Today only the sunsets and the memories remain. But many Lebanese restaurateurs fled the country to set up new ventures in new continents. Consequently it is the Lebanese restaurant in the West that most of us identify with Middle Eastern food. The fact is, though, that the food of all the Levant countries is very similar to that found in the Lebanon.

One of the most celebrated range of dishes is the mezzeh. Famous all over the Middle East, these starter and titbit dishes are especially excellent in the Levant. I describe them in more detail in Chapter Four and they range from simple dishes of olives, nuts or salads to complex dips, cooked items and pastries. Mezzeh are always accompanied by breads such as *kaak* or *khubiz sorj* from the Lebanon, and *sh'raak* in Jordan and Palestine. Another type of bread is *kaark*, a crisp sesame-coated 'bracelet'. Often mezzehs are so satisfying, so many and so filling that you cannot eat any more. But you must find room for the fabulous main courses, of which *kibbeh* is probably regarded as the national dish. The most popular version is spicy ground mutton cooked then stuffed into an outer casing of mince and cracked wheat. Spicy meat dishes are also popular. One creamy dish is *labnah ummo* (lamb cooked in yoghurt), called *mansi* in Palestine, and *samak bil tahine* is Lebanese fish in sesame paste.

There is a wide range of vegetable dishes to choose from including the classic *kossa mashiya* (*kibbeh*-stuffed courgettes), *bamiya* (stir-fried okra) and *fassoolia baydah* (white haricot beans) from Syria. A particularly interesting dish is *roz bi sha'riya*, which combines rice and vermicelli. And if all that was not enough – enter the sweet trolley. Syrupy, honey-laced, nutty pastries such as baklava and *kadayif* cannot be resisted.

THE GULF: SAUDI ARABIA, YEMEN, OMAN, QATAR, KUWAIT, BAHRAIN, UNITED ARAB EMIRATES

The Arabian peninsula is a region of arid waste lands and deserts, punctuated by the occasional water well or oasis. For thousands of years it was home to indigenous tribes who were able to criss-cross those waterless wastes and survive. This in turn presented them with the opportunity to act as the carriers of goods between the Mediterranean and India. They had nothing of their own to trade, but, acting as middle-men, it made the early Arabs extremely wealthy. And with wealth came power. Eventually, in the name of their new-found religion – Islam – they used their wealth and power to become empire builders.

Mohammed was born in the late fifth century AD. He was forty when he founded the Islamic religion, which led to the expansion of the Arab territories in the name of Allah. His followers took Damascus. They captured the Sind (Pakistan) and went on to India and later entered China. They took all the territories of the southern Mediterranean and Spain and they went on into France, occupying the southern half until they were driven out in 732. They had captured Baghdad by 900, at which point their empire was at its height.

It lasted for seven centuries, until it was replaced by a regime it had created itself – the Moslem Ottomans. Arab power waned exactly at the time when their importance as spice traders was supplanted by northern European mariners. Arabia retreated to its peninsula, to insignificance, to poverty and to the old nomadic ways of the Bedouin tribes. And then in this century the hand of fortune caressed Arabia once again. This time it was with oil, and with it has come a rapid and profound change of life style. Bedouin tribes still dwell in the deserts of the Gulf, but today one is more likely to encounter Coca-Cola and Suzukis than camels.

New wealth and high-speed communications have brought burger and pizza bars, luxury hotels and restaurants within reach of all but the most distant townships. Despite that, traditional Arab food is excellent, benefiting from the influences of their foreign trade and conquests. Popular spices in the area include the bitter fenugreek (typified in the dip *hilbeh*), and garlic and chillies are also enjoyed. With their direct links to India, the southern states of the Gulf produce spicy dishes, some very hot, some in curried form. *Kiymeh mashwi*, for example, is a curried mince dish from Oman, derived from the Indian *keema*. *Kafta* (meat balls in spicy gravy) is another dish with an Indo-Persian background. Other Gulf meat and poultry dishes include *kirshuh* (spicy Yemeni offal stir-fry), *djej mechoui* (roast chicken), and *dajaj m'ashi* (stuffed chicken). *Blehal samak* is fish fingers, and *nachbous* is a spicy Kuwaiti prawn stir-fry. Vegetable dishes include *karafsi magaali* (sautéed celery), *korrat bi zayt* (sautéed leeks), and *sheik-el-ma'shi* (courgettes stuffed with mince). *Timman* is Iraqi fried rice, and *khoubiz* is the standard Arab disc-like bread found in one form or another in every country mentioned in this book.

The Arabs have a sweet tooth and enjoy the sticky honey-dripping pastries like baklava and *kunafa*. *Ataif* is a sweet pancake. It is the date, indigenous to the Gulf, which Arabs eat all day and every day in every guise conceivable. *Q'ahwah*, Arab coffee, is also consumed spiced or plain, usually very sweet and always very strong. Twenty cups a day is the norm to the average Arab. But I have left Arabia's most famous dish until last – *khouzi* (whole roast lamb), and its simpler variation, *fakhid kharouf* (roast leg of lamb).

IRAN (PERSIA)

Is it Persia or is it Iran? To find out we must go back over 30,000 years. As the last glacier receded northwards over Europe and Asia, a race of people called 'Indo-Europeans' evolved in the area north of the Caucasian mountains (between the Black Sea and the Caspian mountains). As their population expanded these nomadic tribes branched out, eventually occupying much of Europe, thus becoming the direct ancestors of most modern Europeans. Other branches moved eastwards and by 3000 BC they had settled in the plains of Turkestan, north of Afghanistan. These tribes were called Aryans, and by now they had become cattle herders and dairy farmers. They also invented the horse-drawn war chariot, a weapon which gave them easy victory in their territorial conquests. By 2300 BC a further branch of the tribes, the Parsi-Aryans, entered the land which was to bear derivatives of their tribal name from then on. At first it was called Iran, later it was Parthia or Persia. Over the next 1,500 years the Iranians settled into their lands and perfected the techniques of dairy production. What has endured from these times is the Aryan tradition of cooking with dairy produce, especially yoghurt. It is fundamental to contemporary Indian, Caucasian and Iranian cooking.

In 646 BC the Persian King of the Medes defeated the neighbouring Assyrians, enabling the establishment of the first Persian Empire. It lasted until it was extinguished by Alexander the Great in 323 BC. The Persian Empire made a comeback as Greece declined, and between AD 145 and AD 626 it existed alongside that of Rome, during which time the Persian style of cooking was developed to great heights.

Then came the Arabs and with them Islam. The Persians readily became Moslems, and the Arabs took to Persian cooking, exporting it to all parts of their expanding empire. Persian monarchs continued to rule throughout neighbouring Arab jurisdiction, as they did when the Arabs were ousted by the Ottomans in the fifteenth century. Indeed it was dissatisfaction with generations of autocratic rulers which led to the deposition of the Shah in 1979. It was then that the country was re-named Iran.

Persian food has envolved over very many centuries to produce a very distinctive style. Many dishes have a combination of unlikely ingredients and of sweet, sour and savoury tastes. For example meat marinated in yoghurt is then slowly simmered in pomegranate juice with spices, molasses, honey or sugar and lemon. Whole almonds or pistachio nuts are added. Cooked apricot, peaches, prunes, dates or apples often accompany the principal ingredient. Spicing can also be quite subtle or can predominate, and two good examples of this are *faisanjan* (duck) and *koresh* (spicy stew). Derivatives of the Persian style are found as far apart as Morocco, in *bisteeya* for example, Tunisia (*mishmisheya*), and in Turkey (*tavak koftesi*). Variations of the *kofte* meatball dish are favourites in most Arab lands, and they are also found in India, imported there by the Persian and Arab invaders.

The art of rice cooking almost certainly began in Persia. *Pollou* gave birth to the many similar Middle Eastern rice dishes. *Chellow* is a rice favourite, and *tahig* is the tasty crisp rice crust which is allowed to form whilst cooking *chellow*. *Nane lavash* is a thin, floppy Iranian bread, whilst *lavash* is very crisp.

TURKEY

The earliest civilized settlers in Anatolia (Turkey) were a tribe called the Hittites, who had become established by 2500 BC. By 480 BC the area had become part of the enormous Persian Empire. This fell to Greece by

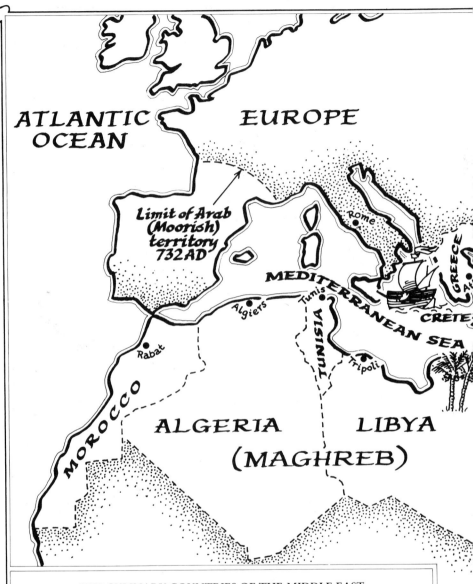

ATLANTIC
OCEAN

EUROPE

Limit of Arab
(Moorish)
territory
732 AD

Rome

MEDITERRANEAN SEA

GREECE

CRETE

Algiers

Tunis

TUNISIA

Rabat

Tripoli

MOROCCO

ALGERIA

LIBYA

(MAGHREB)

THE CULINARY COUNTRIES OF THE MIDDLE EAST

The countries of our culinary Middle East spread a total of 4,200 miles (6,720 km) from west (Morocco) to east (Iran) and 2,200 miles (3,520 km) north (Turkey) to south (Yemen). It has a total area of 4.6 million square miles, and a population of 227 million. (The USA, by comparison, spans some 3,000 miles by 1,600 miles, has an area of 3.6 million miles and a population of 200 million.) In terms of longitude the span is 13°W to 63°E and latitude 10°N to 43°N with most of the landmasses being located at around 30°. Climatically therefore, it is hot, and much of the land is very arid desert.

323 BC. Later Anatolia became Christian, and Constantinople a major Roman trading centre. As the Roman Empire declined it divided into two, and in AD 629 the eastern division became Byzantium. In 1071 it fell to Moslems who invaded from the Levant.

The original Turks were descendants of the ancient Aryan tribes, inhabiting the area of the USSR still called Turkestan. By AD 550 they had become powerful enough to control a kingdom. Over the next 500 years their power base extended, and they became Moslem.

By 1400 it was the Turkish Ottomans who controlled eastern Greece and Turkey. That empire continued to expand over the next 400 years until they controlled all the countries I've talked about in this book with the exception of Morocco and Persia. The beginning of this century saw an Ottoman Empire intact but suffering from a feudal sultanate wracked with indecision, corruption and mistakes, epitomized by its leaders (for no good reason) siding with the losers of World War I. The outcome was the dismantling of their empire in 1919, its territories being divided between Britain and France. The country was named Turkey for the first time. (Throughout the Ottoman period the word 'Turk' was synonymous with 'barbarian tribesman', a deep insult.) A series of major cultural reforms was enforced, and Islam was disbanded, as was the Arabic script. Most Turks are Moslem but do not strictly adhere to Islam's tenets: alcohol is enjoyed and the veil non-existent.

The powerful and long-lived Ottoman Empire was one of the world's most colourful, brutal and despotic regimes. Its sultans enjoyed all the comforts that their wealth and power could afford. Their palaces glittered with gold and jewels, and their harems and belly dancers are renowned. But perhaps the greatest legacy is their food. It is arguably the best and most imaginative of all the countries in this book, even surpassing (but only just) that of Morocco. The names of some of the dishes themselves indicate what was on the sultans' minds, when their chefs created them for their masters. Dishes such as 'Ladies' Navels', 'Ladies' Thighs', 'Sweet Lips', 'Dainty Fingers' and 'Turkish Delight' regularly appeared at court and are still Turkish favourites.

Restaurant tradition is fairly new to Turkey, but entertaining at home is traditional and sometimes very lavish. Mezzeh features largely on such occasions, as described in Chapter Four, and the array of dishes is virtually endless. Even the table on which they are served, the 'Raki table', sums up Turkish enjoyment of mezzeh. *Raki* is a locally produced aniseed liqueur, and is a seemingly indispensable accompaniment to Turkish mezzeh.

Taramasalata, a fish roe dip, is probably one of the best-known Greek/Turkish mezzeh dishes. Other representative Turkish dishes include *kiymail yumarta* (minced meat topped with egg), *kestaneli hindi guveci* (turkey casseroled with chestnuts) and *pilich dolmesi* (boned stuffed chicken). There is a wealth of fish dishes including *kilich shish* (skewered sword fish). *Sardalya* and *hamsi tavasi* are pan-fried sardines and anchovies respectively, and *baliklar koftesi* is fish balls. *Istakoz firinda* is a fine baked lobster dish. There are dozens of vegetable dishes of unsurpassed quality.

Khave turki (Turkish coffee), as with the Arab nations, is a way of life with the Turks. Tiny cups of very thick strong coffee are drunk at any time of the day, usually black and frequently with a lot of sugar. Even more popular than coffee is *chaiy turki* (Turkish tea), which is also readily available. Street vendors carry polished brass 'back-pack' urns to dispense coffee or tea to paying passers-by. A similar urn, this time glass, dispenses *visine*, a sour cherry drink or lemonade.

Finally mention must be made of that world-famous confectionery, *lokum*, better known as Turkish Delight. Naturally pale coloured, it is made from grape pulp with semolina and gelatine, and icing sugar is sprinkled on after it is set.

THE CAUCASIAN COUNTRIES: ARMENIA, AZERBAIJAN AND GEORGIA

Geographically, the Caucasian mountains, which stretch from the Black Sea to the Caspian, form a natural divide. To the south now lie Turkey and Iran and the Pontic mountains. (It was on the highest peak of these mountains, the 17,000-foot Mount Ararat, that the Old Testament tells us Noah beached his Ark after the flood.) A sub-race called the Caucasians evolved north of the mountains and by 4500 BC they had expanded to occupy the Levant, Turkey and parts of Greece and Iran. Later they were pushed back to their original home lands, which had become part of the Persian Empire by 646 BC. By Greek times the Kingdom of Armenia was established, and in AD 303 it became the world's first Christian state, preceding Rome itself by 34 years. With the decline of the Roman Empire, Armenia was absorbed into the expanding Persian Empire. It re-emerged as an independent kingdom by AD 650, but fell victim to Arab ascendency in 717. Armenia and Azerbaijan, under Moslem Emirs, turned largely to Islam, but the tiny kingdom of Abasgia (later called Georgia), remained the sole centre of the Eastern Church despite becoming a part of the Russian Empire in 1783.

In culinary terms the food is an individual combination of Arab and Turkish styles. Whilst it is not impossible today to visit the Russian Republics of Armenia, Azerbaijan and Georgia, it is more likely that one will encounter their food in the few restaurants run by ex-patriot Armenians in the West. My recipe selection includes the outstanding poultry dish *cerkez tavagu* (chicken cooked in a paste of paprika, walnuts, garlic and oil), which is regarded as the national dish. Bulgar is a version of burghul (cracked wheat), used in cooking and salads. *Uskumru plaki* is mackerel casserole, *bras yahni* a dish of sautéed leeks. Chickpeas make their appearance in *nivig* (with spinach), and this served cold is especially favoured during the non-meat-eating period of Lent.

Highly specialized items, best left to the professionals as they require skill and hot sun to make (but obtainable occasionally at specialist delicatessens), are dried meats and sausages. *Aboukht* is beef, seasoned with salt and a fenugreek paste, dried in the sun. It is called pastrami in neighbouring Soviet countries and *pastrouma* in Greece, Turkey and Israel. Mortadella is a spicy lamb or mutton sausage with old Italian links, which also manifest themselves in the form of the Armenian pastas *rishata* and *arshta. With its Aryan and Persian links, mazdoon* (yoghurt) is widely used, particularly in the yoghurt drink *tam*, which is similar to *abdug*.

GREECE AND CYPRUS

Historically Greece is probably best remembered for its ancient empire which, by 323 BC, was at its height under Alexander the Great, claiming territory from India to Spain. That empire gave way to Rome, then by AD 650 Greece was partly in the hands of Byzantium, Rome's eastern replacement, while central Greece fell into the hands of a tribe called the Avar Huns, later known as the Bulgars. By around 1000 the Byzantines had recovered most of Greece and Turkey; but they were gradually to lose Turkey and shrink back into Greece. By 1453 Byzantium was finally totally wiped out and the whole of Greece was incorporated into the Turkish Ottoman Empire. It was not until the nineteenth century that the kingdom of Greece was established in the south of the country, and by 1912 it had taken back all of Greece from Turkey, establishing it once and for all in Europe. Centuries of Arab–Turkish culture and Islam were finally expelled in favour of Christianity. Politically enmity remains to this day, highlighted in divided Cyprus.

Although modern Greece is not part of the Middle East, its strong links over the centuries are too strong to ignore. At first I had decided to omit Greek and Cypriot recipes because so many of their dishes owe their origins to Turkey. But it is not quite as simple as that. Certain dishes originated long before Turkish Moslem occupation and are directly attributable to Byzantine influences. Certain other Greek dishes owe their origins to the Turkish Ottomans. As a general rule, Greek dishes are mellower than Turkish, spices being used but to a lesser extent. The many dishes which share names, such as mezzeh (itself derived from a Greek word), dolmas (stuffed items), *pilafis* (rice dishes), the savoury and sweet filo (stuffed pastry items), the use of yoghurt (*jiarouru*) and the strong, thick, sweet coffee will be found not only in Greece and Turkey but in much of the Arab world in one form or another. I have decided to omit most recipes that are found only in Greece.

Three Greek dishes that I have included because they are so delicious are *spanokopitta*, little filo pastry pies with spinach and feta cheese, and its two variations, *tyropitta* and *kotopitta*, the first with egg and cheese filling and the second with minced chicken.

TOWN LIFE

The Arab town and city is a vibrant, colourful hive of activity, bustle, noise, and social encounter. People scurry from place to place about their business, or sit in laughing, talkative groups at street cafés, relaxing over endless cups of coffee and titbits (the women apart from the men).

In the Arab heartlands, dress is almost wholly traditional – the men in white or coloured robes and elegant headdresses, the women always in *yashmaks*, often in black. The sun beats down, the streets are none too clean, the smells mingle, some pleasant, some not. Motor vehicles clatter past, horns shrieking endlessly; donkeys, camels, mules and bullocks piled high with wares plod wearily by; lean cats and dogs seek scraps, whilst exotic city birds flash from pole to pole.

No matter how large and modern the city, it always has its market or *soukh*, *kazbah* or *medina*. Whether the city is Cairo or Tangiers, Istanbul or Jeddah, Baghdad or Tehran, it is usually walled and very ancient, and inside it is like going back in time. Motor vehicles are usually not permitted into the maze of twisting lanes between tall buildings. But it is the dozens, sometimes hundreds of market traders that form the main interest of the *soukh*. Nothing has changed for centuries. It is a place for buying and selling and every conceivable commodity is there: pots, pans, clothing, perfume, ornaments, jewellery, flowers, livestock, fish, meat, vegetables, groceries, freshly baked bread, yoghurt, cheese and milk. There is rarely a stall – the trader just selects a place to stand or sit. Often there is precious little on sale. This man may be trying to sell one scrawny goat, that man may have a few saucepans on offer. This heavily veiled woman may have a few freshly picked carrots for sale and that one, some yoghurt in earthenware pots. These people come in from their villages from time to time in order to earn their keep for a few days. People shout and haggle, traders call their wares, money and goods change hands. It is all colour and action, it is unmissable.

RELIGION AND DIETARY TABOOS

The world's oldest monotheistic religion – Judaism – was born in the Middle East as early as 2000 BC, with the establishment of Abraham's wandering tribe. The formalized growth of Judaism did not take place until around 800 BC, some 300 years after the establishment of Israel (the Old Testament was not written until around 300 BC). Judaism, the basis of Christianity and Islam, is practised today by about 12 million people, half of whom are in the USA and 4 million in Israel.

Christianity also originated in Israel and there are some 25 million Christians in the Middle East. The first converts were the Egyptians: today's descendants, who can trace their ancestry back to Pharaonic times, are Copt Christians. Armenia was converted in AD 303, Rome followed in 337, then Turkey and Greece, and these nations, with the exception of

Rome, belong to the Eastern Orthodox faith, whose centre is Istanbul. There is another pocket of Christianity in the Lebanon.

The third religion to come out of the Middle East was Islam, Arabia being its birthplace. Of the 227 million people in the Middle East, 87 per cent are Moslem. Put into perspective, there are, world-wide, 1 billion Christians, $\frac{1}{2}$ billion Hindus, 350 million Moslems and 200 million Buddhists.

Both Judaism and Islam have certain taboos about food. The Jews must only eat food which is Kosher, fit and proper, whilst Moslems must only eat food which is Halal, clean. To fail to do so would be unthinkable to true practitioners of both religions. Kosher and Halal food must be prepared and eaten according to unbreakable rules: meat must be slaughtered then cut in a particular way and blood must not be present in the meat ready for cooking. Common to both religions is the proscription on the eating of pork. Jews may not eat invertebrates such as shellfish and snails, although this does not apply to Moslems. Jews may not cook on their weekly day of rest, the Sabbath, but they may eat. Moslems may not eat between sun up and sun down during their month-long fast of Ramadan. Moslems still practise ritual sacrifice (eg, of a lamb or kid), Christians must practise abstention during their month-long period of Lent, and they are supposed not to eat red meat on Fridays, in memory of the Crucifixion.

COOKING METHODS AND UTENSILS

Most of the population of the Middle East live in primitive conditions. Running water, gas or electricity will only be found in the largest villages. The average Western kitchen, with its smart work-surfaces, its oven and four-ring stove, hot and cold water, freezer, fridge, dish washer, food processor, blender and microwave, would seem like a space ship. Even in the larger cities, the middle class will not possess more than the basic 'mod-cons', but, despite this, any Middle Eastern cook seems able to produce magnificent fare from the most limited resources.

Most homes still rely on a single burner, often a meths primus (*fatayel*) on which to cook, but many use their hearth or a simple charcoal or wood fire. Timing and technique enables the cook to prepare several dishes at the same time on the single heat source. A facility, which does not exist in the West, but which transforms their cooking is the availability of the local bakery (*furunji*). The baker (*furun*) not only makes bread to sell, but his charcoal-fired ovens can be used by the locals. Rather like a service wash at the launderette, the cook simply takes her dish to the *furun*, who, for a few pennies, will casserole stews, turning them, stirring, even adding any ingredients supplied, or bake cakes, pastries, or bread from the customer's own dough, who can either return for the completed item at an agreed time, or may stay at the bakery enjoying the company of friends over cups of coffee until her cooking is ready. The *furunji* is not just practical, it is an enjoyable meeting place.

The Middle Eastern cook possesses a round baking dish called *tapsi* in Greece and *sanieh* in Arabic, and a lidded casserole dish, *tsoukali*. Other utensils include pottery dishes, copper pans (now giving way to aluminium) and a cast iron or steel frying pan, usually shaped like a wok. Everyone has a mortar and pestle, and a special long-handled pot to make the ubiquitous Arab style coffee. There is a wicker or woven basket through which to strain yoghurt, and for specialist dishes there are certain specialist utensils to match. The Egyptian bean dish, *ful medames* requires a double boiler in the cylindrical tapering top of which the beans slowly cook. The North African couscous is cooked in a utensil of different shape but similar concept called the *couscousière*, and there are special rice cookers. None of this need daunt the western cook, who will be perfectly able to prepare and cook any of the recipes in this book without specialist equipment.

MEALS OF THE DAY

Most Middle Eastern people eat three meals a day. Breakfast is traditionally lighter than lunch and dinner. A typical breakfast might include *labnah* (yoghurt cheese) spiced with *za'atar*, a blend of powdered herbs. Olives and dates, plain or stuffed, and fresh fruit, honey and nuts are usually present. Freshly baked Arab bread is stacked high, and is used to scoop up the selection of food. Eggs in a variety of forms are favourites.

The main meal of the day can be at the middle of the day, but it usually is served in the evening when the family is together. It consists of perhaps three dishes, which probably include meat, poultry or fish, and one or two vegetable dishes. A grain dish, often rice, and bread are the staples and there will undoubtedly be relishes, yoghurt and a salad. The main course is followed by fruit and nuts, sweets, pastries and coffee.

The lighter meal of the day will often consist of a selection of mezzeh.

Between meals, 'picking' is regarded as the norm and of course the strong, thick coffee or tea is always bubbling away.

At meal times the men of the family are fed first. They take the best of the food and what is left is then eaten by the women and children – often in another room, whilst the men smoke their hubble-bubble pipes. The meal is taken seated on cushions around a low table or carpet. Before eating, a large ornate tray with matching bowl and jug, often made from hand-beaten copper, silver or even, for the wealthiest, gold, is brought in by one of the women. The bowl contains warm soapy water and the jug, just water. The ritual is that both hands are washed, rinsed and dried before eating can commence.

The meal itself is served in large communal bowls. The diner selects the items of his own choice with his right hand only, and eats with it, using, in most Islamic countries, the thumb and first two fingers up to the second knuckle. Only at the end of the meal is it polite to lick the fingers.

Westernized Middle Easterners, of course, are quite happy to use cutlery, but it was a former Shah who said 'eating with a knife and fork is like making love through an interpreter'.

A guest at a Middle Eastern home must never be refused hospitality, no matter how inconvenient. The ubiquitous Arab coffee is offered first, followed by snacks (or mezzeh). The guest for his or her part must refuse these offerings at the time of asking. He will be asked again and even a third time. He must not actually refuse, but eventually accept 'under pressure'. Not to go through this ritual would seem highly impolite.

ALCOHOL

Alcohol is strictly forbidden to Moslems. In most of the Gulf countries, even non-Moslems are subject to severe punishment – public floggings, for instance – if discovered having a tipple even in the privacy of their own homes.

Some Moslem countries are far more tolerant about alcohol, particularly those with a burgeoning tourist trade, or those with Christian populations. Many of the wines and spirits produced in these countries are now available in the West. If you can get hold of a locally produced bottle, it adds great interest to your meal.

Morocco

The vineyards are post-war French plantings. *Vin Gris de Boulaoune* and *Gris de Guerrovane* are pale dry rosés, *Sidi Larbi* and *Dar bel Amri* are reds. *L'Oustalet* is a white blanc de blanc. *Mahia* is a liqueur made from dates and figs.

Tunisia

By contrast the Tunisian vineyards are very ancient, many originating from 400 BC and the days of Carthage. *Muscat de Keliba* and *Château Khanguet* are good whites, and *Magon* and *Sidi Saad* are good reds. *Boukha* is a fig liqueur, *Thibar* a sweet brandy, and *sirop* is an ultra-sweet pomegranate liqueur. On the island of Jerba, *la'hmi* is a sour fermented date liqueur.

Algeria

The French influence has enabled Algeria to produce a series of fine rosés and reds from the Mascara, Medea and Dahra regions and reds from Zaccar and Tessala.

Egypt

It was the Pharaohs who first developed the art of wine-making in Egypt.

Early this century new Egyptian vineyards were established near Alexandria at Abu Hummus. Two good whites are *Reine Cléopatre* and *Cru des Ptolemées*. *Omar Khayyam* is a smooth red with a hint of the flavour of dates. *Arak*, also called *Zibib*, is a spirit distilled from wine and flavoured with aniseed.

The Levant
Vineyards were established in 1857 by Jesuits in the Bekaa valley at Ksara. Two good wines from there are *Château Kefraya* (rosé) and *Château Musar* (red). *Arak* is also produced. There are also small vineyards in Syria at Halab, Homs and near Damascus and in Jordan at Az-Zarqa and Ram.

Israel
Baron Edmond de Rothschild laid down extensive vineyards at Mount Carmel near Tel Aviv in 1880 at the time when his French château Bordeaux had reached the peak of excellence. Today a range of reds includes *Vin Fou*, *Avat* and the sweet *Adon Atic*, and white wines include *Carmel Hock* and the drier *Château de la Montague*. Sparkling wines are produced and there are even *kosher* wines.

Turkey
Turkey is the biggest wine producer in the Moslem world. Indeed its vineyard average is the world's fifth largest, although many of the grapes are eaten as fruit. The celebrated Turkish wines are a light red *Trakya*, from Thrace, and a robust dark red *Buzbag* from Anatolia. There is also a white *Trakya*. *Tckirdag* is a medium white. *Raki* is the Turkish version of *Arak*, drunk in Turkey with *mezzeh*. *Mersin* is a liqueur made from oranges.

Armenia
Archaeological evidence shows that Armenia invented wine-making over 3,500 years ago. The tradition has been maintained to this day and the area produces some of the Soviet Union's best wines. Exports occasionally reach the West and are worth trying for curiosity value alone. Armenia is also a major producer of sherry, brandy and vodka. *Oghi* is similar to Turkish *Raki* and Lebanese *Arak*.

CHAPTER 2

A MIDDLE EASTERN MENU

CONSTRUCTING your Middle Eastern menu is great fun. The range of options is enormous. I have organized the subsequent chapters into groups so that you can create a meal of one, two, three or even four courses by bringing together your choice of dishes from the relevant chapters. Equally you can put together a selection of snacks or quickly make a single light supper (or even breakfast).

If you wish, you can put together representative dishes of one country or area. Alternatively, and I think quite legitimately, your meal will be even more interesting if you construct your menu using the dishes of many 'Middle Eastern' countries. They are all compatible. Here are a few menu examples doing it either way. You can find their recipes by consulting the index.

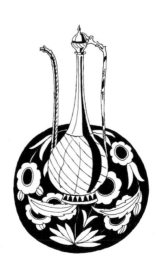

A Menu from Maghreb

Starter
Shorba bil hout (fish soup)

Main Course
Couscous (steamed semolina grains) served with Chicken
tagine (stew)
Batata ma'li (spicy potato) served with Harissa (chilli dip)
Green salad
Limoon makbous (pickled lemons)

Dessert
M'hancha (snake cake)
Chai bi na'na (mint tea)

A Menu from Egypt

Starter
Felafel (chickpea croquette)
Fattoush (mixed salad with bread)

Main Course
Siman bil kibbeh (quail stuffed with wheat)
Melokhia (green vegetables)
Ful nabed (broad beans) served with Aiysh (bread),
Mixed salad and
Taratoor b'sade (garlic dip)
M'qalel (pickled vegetables)

Dessert
Um m'ali (Ali's mum's pud)
Q'ahwa Arabiya (Arab coffee)

A Menu from Israel

Starter
Sabra dip (avocado dip) with Pastelle (puff pastry pot)

Main Course
Cholent (casseroled beef/lamb)
Mixed vegetables
Latkes (shredded potato cakes) served with Bagels (crusty
bread rings)

Dessert
Tea or coffee with Sephardi (stuffed dates)

A Menu from the Levant

Starter (mezzeh)
Kibid mili (sautéed lamb liver)
Tabouleh (cracked wheat salad)
Shashlik kebabs (grilled lamb on skewers) served with
Khoubiz or Ka'ak (bread)

Main Course
Kibbeyets (stuffed meat in burghul)
Bamiya b'zayt (stir-fried okra)
Roz bi sha'riyah (rice and vermicelli)
Torshi (pickled vegetables)

Dessert
Sujee helva (fried semolina pudding)

A Menu from Arabia

Starter
Dukkah (a crumbly dip)
Loubia b'zeyt (green bean salad)
Nachbous (shrimps)

Main Course
Fakhid kharouf (roast lamb)
Ads bi Gibba (brown lentils) served with Khoubiz (bread)

Dessert
Kadayif (sweet crisp shredded pastries)
Q'ahwa Arabiya (Arab coffee)

A Hot and Spicy Menu from Yemen and Oman

Starter
Kirshuh (heart, kidney and liver stir-fry)
Sambusak boregi (small stuffed pastry)
Labnah makbous (yoghurt cheese in oil)

Main Course
Kiymeh mashwi omani (spicy minced meat)
or Djej mechoui (spicy roast chicken)
Sheik-el-ma'shi (stuffed courgettes)
Hilbeh (fenugreek hot dip)
Chellow with Hakkakah (rice with a crispy crust)
or Saluf bi hilbeh (spicy bread)
Qali filfil (vinegared chillies)

Dessert
Ataif (syrupy pancake)
Q'shr (yemeni coffee)

A Menu from Iran

Starter
Kookoo sabzi (herbal omelette)
Sabzi isfahan khodran (mint and herb salad)
Abdug (yoghurt drink)

Main Course
Faisinjan (duck in pomegranate)
Houmous ye esfanaj (chickpeas and spinach)
Chellow (rice)
Limoon makbous (pickled lemons)

Dessert
Fresh fruit
Tea with Loze hilou (sugared nuts)

A Menu from Turkey

Starter
Midye izmiri tavasi (fried mussels)

Main Course
Kastelani hindi guveci (turkey and chestnuts)
Enginar (artichokes)
Tereyagli kereviz (sautéed celery)
Beyaz pilav (white rice)
Biber tursu (vinegared chillies)

Dessert
Kadayif (sweet shredded pastries)
Chaiy turki (Turkish tea) and Lokum (Turkish Delight)

A Menu of Middle Eastern Favourites

(Suitable for a party)

Starter (mezzeh)
Houmous b'tahine (chickpea dip) – Levant
Taramasalata (fish roe dip) – Turkey
Dolmades (stuffed vine leaves) – Greece
Felafel (chickpea rissoles) – Israel
Boreks and Breiks (pastries) – Turkey/Maghreb

Main Course
M'choui (whole spicy roast lamb) – Morocco
Lahma-kafta bil karaz (lamb and cherry kofta) – Saudi
Masgouf (baked curried fish) – Iraq
Ful medamis (brown beans) – Egypt
Chakchouka (ratatouille-style vegetables) – Maghreb
Pollou (rice) – Iran
Pitta (Turkey) and Khoubiz (Saudi) breads
Tursusu (pickled vegetables)

Dessert
Baklava, Kadayif and fresh fruit
Mint Tea, Coffee and Turkish Delight

CHAPTER 3

BASIC INGREDIENTS AND RECIPES

IN THIS chapter I have collected together information about basic flavouring ingredients. Middle Eastern cooking uses herbs quite extensively. Spices vary from country to country. The southern Gulf states such as the Yemen and Oman use a lot of spices, especially hot ones. In northern Iraq and Tunisia, pungent spices such as chilli and fenugreek are popular, whilst in Morocco, cummin, cinnamon and pepper make frequent appearances. Saffron is the prize of the Arabs, is used in many fragrant recipes, and garlic is a universal flavourer. Nuts are important for both taste and texture, walnuts being the Caucasian favourite, hazelnuts being used in Turkey and Morocco; almonds are generally popular, especially in Iran, as are pistachios; pine nuts are the favourite in the Levant and the Gulf.

There are a number of spice mixtures used in different countries and these are described in this chapter, and used in subsequent recipes. In some countries much cooking is done in olive oil or clarified butter called *smen*. But a number of other oils are used to good effect, and these are examined here.

Yoghurt plays a vital part in the Middle East. It is used as a dip and a sauce to cook with, and as a refreshing drink in hot countries where alcohol is forbidden. It is also made into cheese. I have included recipes for these and for another Middle Eastern favourite, pickles.

FRESH HERBS

Fresh herbs are used imaginatively in the Middle East. Some are familiar and easily obtained in the West, others are never available. A wander around any *soukh* will reveal heaps and heaps of colourful fragrant herbs of so many varieties that it would be impractical to list them all, if indeed that were possible, as some seem not to have English translations. The following list is therefore a mere whiff of the delights of the Arabian herb garden: basil, chervil, coriander, cress (*barbeen*), dill, fennel, garlic, chives, marjoram, *melokhia*, mint, parsley, purslane, rosemary, sage and thyme.

For more information about these herbs please refer to the Herbs section on page 177.

SPICES

Nowhere in the world uses more spices in its cuisine than the sub-continent of India. Second is the Middle East. This is not surprising considering the close historical links between the Arabian Moslems, Persia and India. Most spices are common to the three, and it leads to a close similarity in taste with some dishes. Curry will not be found in the Middle East, although some dishes are not far removed. In particular, the spicy Iranian meat or vegetable spicy stew *koresh* is not unlike curry (indeed it could be that the Iranian word *koresh* gave 'curry' its name).

The following are some of the most important cooking spices used in the various Middle Eastern countries: allspice, aniseed, barberry, bay leaves, caraway, cardamom (green), cassia, chilli, clove, coriander, cummin, fenugreek, ginger, *mahlab*, nutmeg, paprika, pomegranate, poppy seed, saffron, sesame, *sumaq*, turmeric and *za'atar*.

For more information about these spices please refer to the Spices section on page 179.

Middle Eastern spice mixtures

Unlike Indian dishes, which mostly use several, sometimes many, spices whole and/or ground, Middle Easterners more often use just one or two to flavour their dishes. But some of their dishes use combinations of spices, and these reflect the taste preferences of the various countries. In each the choice of spices and the proportions vary widely, depending on the preference of the individual cook. The following mixtures should be regarded, therefore, as representative rather than definitive.

Bahar

Widely used ground mixture of three sweetish spices, cinnamon, clove and nutmeg. Sometimes a pinch of ginger and/or pepper is added. When allspice was brought to the Middle East from the Americas in the sixteenth century, its flavour was so similar that it was given the name *bahar* and virtually replaces it.

Baharat

An Arab mixture of ground spices, normally including a combination of cinammon, clove, coriander, cummin, nutmeg, paprika (for colour) and pepper.

Chermoula or Tchermila
A marinating paste made by grinding to a purée 1 onion, 2–4 cloves garlic, 1 cup parsley or coriander, 2–4 red chillies or 1–2 teaspoons chilli powder, 4 teaspoons paprika, 1 teaspoon salt, 1 teaspoon ground pepper and 1 teaspoon saffron.

La Kama
From Tangiers in Morocco. To flavour soups and stews, typically including ground spices to the following proportions: 2 parts black pepper to 2 ginger, 1 turmeric, 1 cinnamon and $\frac{1}{4}$ nutmeg.

Lebanese Mixture
A simple mixture of ground spices which can be used at the early stages of cooking soups or stews, or as a condiment sprinkled on the finished dish: 2 parts cinammon to 2 paprika and 1 chilli.

Ras El Hanout
The most celebrated Moroccan spice mix, containing a mixture of around twenty (sometimes twenty-five) whole spices, dried herbs and flowers; it literally means 'shop-keepers' choice', and there are as many variants as there are Moroccan spice sellers. It is a familiar sight in the markets, where the spice vendor will sell it by the teaspoon, kilo or sack. As each vendor has his own secret blend passed down by word of mouth over generations, there are innumerable permutations of ingredients. The ingredients list is, as you would suspect, not at all easy to extract from the salesman – even if one does, it is not always easy to understand what they tell you in Arabic. I met a very bizarre trader who sat crosslegged on his mat in the spice market (*souk-el-attarine*) in Tetuane, and as far as I could tell from my interpreter friend, this was what his *ras-el-hanout* contained: spices – peppercorns (black and white), chilli, cummin, coriander, cassia, nutmeg, whole green cardamom, cloves, mace, fenugreek, black cummin; dried flower petals – rosebuds, orange blossom, lemon blossom, belladonna berries, saffron, German iris, lavender; cantharides (Spanish Fly); Roots – ginger, galingale (lesser), wall broomgrass (*tharra*), rhizome of ash tree; herbs – rosemary, thyme, *harmel*, *jusquiane*, grains of paradise, java almond (*bsibsa*).

The end result is used to flavour such dishes as *tagine*, and its use is said to increase vigour, health, and longevity, not to mention virility.

Ta'leyah or Taqliya
A mix of onion fried with garlic used as a garnish, chutney or baked on bread (see page 53). A Yemeni variant, *talia*, includes chilli.

Tahine or Tahini
Tahine is almost regarded as a staple, and is simple to make. Sesame seeds are lightly roasted, then they are ground and mixed with sesame or olive

oil to make a smooth, stiff paste. Salt and garlic can be included optionally. *Tahine* is available canned or bottled from commercial sources, but the quality differs widely. It is used in many ways in cooking.

Za'atar
This is the Arabic word for thyme. It can also mean a blend of powdered herbs and spices, which usually includes thyme, marjoram, *sumak* and roasted sesame seeds.

Zhug
From Yemen, where they like hot spices, this is a mixture of ground cummin, cardamom and garlic, which are fried, and chilli and herbs such as fresh coriander, which are blanched. Combine and grind to a paste. Used as a chutney within a day or two, or with vinegar added, it keeps.

DRIED FRUIT
Dried fruit such as dates, figs, apricots and plums are particularly popular used in cooking.

OLIVES
The olive is one of the earliest known 'fruits'. Originally a native of the Mediterranean, there are many varieties, differing in size, quality, colour and taste. The difference between whitish, green, purple and black olives is simply the degree of ripeness. Eaten raw, they are too bitter to be palatable. Treated by prolonged immersion in brine or vinegar they became the familiar item. In all the countries of the Middle East they are consumed with great satisfaction – plain, stuffed or in cooking.

NUTS
Five nuts figure prominently in the Middle East, and all are indigenous to the area. Almonds are used in Iranian and Turkish food. The Iraqis use hazelnuts, and walnuts will be found in Armenian and Georgian food. These nuts are used whole or crushed in both savoury and sweet cooked dishes and in salads. Less familiar in the West are pine nuts (*snorbeh*), small, flat, cream-coloured ovals which, after roasting, give a distinctive nutty taste when added to the cooking pot, and are especially popular in Egypt, Syria and the Lebanon. The pistachio nut is green with touches of purple on the outside, and inside it is creamy and succulent. It's best used as a garnish for sweet and savoury dishes because, although used in Middle Eastern cooking, unless added at the last minute its flavour becomes 'stewed in' and wasted. Used in Iranian rice it is particularly tasty.

OILS AND FATS

There are a number of different oils and fats used in the Middle East.

Olive Oil

This is extensively used for cooking and salads, especially in the north of the region, in Greece, Turkey and the Levant. It has a powerful taste when used in cooking.

Sesame Oil

This has been used since ancient times, and indeed it is still a favourite with the Egyptian Copts and many others. It has a very distinctive taste, and prolonged cooking sweetens it.

Smen or Samneh

This is butter, which is heated to clarify it. When allowed to cool it sets to a dripping-like consistency. Its colour ranges from pure white to deep yellow and it has a delicious aroma which is imparted to food, especially subtle dishes such as rice. It is usually made from goat's or sheep's butter, occasionally camel's. If made from from cow's butter it is indistinguishable from Indian *ghee*. It was almost certainly an invention of the cattle breeding Aryans, who took it to India and the Middle East. When cooled and set, it will keep for several months. *Smen* can be made from block margarine.

It is easy to make. Simply bring a couple of packs of ordinary butter to the boil then turn down the heat, and simmer for half an hour or so on the lowest heat. Strain it into a container, discarding the sediment. Apart from the wonderful flavour, its great advantage is that, having no impurities, it can be heated to a higher temperature than other oils, and food cooked in it is less likely to burn. Vegetable ghee is a cheaper substitute with similar properties to *samneh*, but less flavour. All are highly saturated.

Alya

This is a type of dripping made from the tails of a particular breed of sheep or lamb. The trunk of the animal has little fat, but its tail carries a huge fat reserve – sometimes as much as 30lb (13·5kg) in weight – which is usually rendered into dripping. For certain special uses such as the doner kebab, the fat is cut into long, thin strips. Its use in the modern Middle East has sharply declined recently, although some still regard it as essential for flavour. Any meat dripping can be substituted.

Other Oils

Any oil is suitable for cooking. Vegetable or corn oils are inexpensive and neutrally flavoured. For the health-conscious, light mono- or poly-unsaturated oils such as sunflower or soya should be used. *Samneh*, *ghee* and dripping congeal of course, so are unsuitable for salads or cold dishes. Hazelnut and walnut oils are, in my view, two of the most delightful aromatic oils available and are perfect for salads. They are quite expensive and their subtlety is lost in cooking.

GARLIC (*Thawm* or *Tum*)

Garlic probably originated in Turkestan and Siberia. The ancient Egyptians valued it highly, believing that a bulb of garlic represented the cosmos, and each clove parts of the solar system. It was fundamental to their diet, and 15lb (6·75kg) of garlic would buy one slave. Indeed an inscription on the Great Pyramid of Cheops states that the slave builders were supplied garlic and radishes daily for health. History's first recorded industrial dispute took place 3,000 years before Christ, when these slaves mustered up the courage to go on strike because their garlic ration was cut. Garlic was found in Tutankhamun's tomb, and it also had a large role to play in warding off the evil eye.

The Babylonians of 3000 BC considered garlic to be miraculous especially medicinally, as did the Greeks. In 460 BC Hippocrates extolled its virtues, as did Aristotle eighty years later, and Aristophanes believed it enhanced virility. The Phoenicians carried garlic in their Mediterranean trading ships and the Talmudic Kosher rules of the Hebrews proscribe when and where garlic may be used. Mohammed respected garlic: amongst other things, he recommended its use to counteract the stings and bites of venomous creatures such as scorpions. It is said he delighted in eating raw onion and garlic. Yet he warned that they could have powerful aphrodisiac qualities, and had a vision of Satan in the Garden of Eden with onion on the ground at his left foot and garlic at his right.

Garlic is indispensable to the life-style of today's Middle East. It grows everywhere, it is used in raw and cooked dishes, sometimes subtly, sometimes overpoweringly. It even appears in certain sweet dishes.

YOGHURT

Yoghurt predates history, and how it came to be invented can only be speculation. It is milk into which a culture or bacteria is introduced at a controlled heat to cause fermentation, souring and coagulation. New yoghurt can be started by using some existing yoghurt as the culture. It is a chicken and egg story. So how did the first yoghurt start? One theory is that the ancient tribes, probably the dairy-farming Aryans, carried their spare milk in leather pouches. Some bacteria may have got into the pouch and the heat of the Middle Eastern sun did the rest.

Today it is almost a staple all over the area. It is known as *laban* in Arabia, Egypt and Levant, as *mast* in Iran, *mazdoon* in Armenia and *jiaouru* in Greece. *Labnah* is the Arabian version of yoghurt cheese, simply made by straining ordinary yoghurt through muslin overnight and shaping the soft curds into balls. Taken at breakfast in Armenia this is called *banir* and *peynir* in Turkey, and these are closely related to India's *paneer*.

HOME-MADE YOGHURT

Making yoghurt is a skill well worth mastering. Not only does home-made yoghurt cost a fraction of factory versions, but it is fresher and creamier too. To start a yoghurt you need fresh milk (not UHT) or powdered milk. You also need a live bacteriological culture called *bulgaris*, to start the process. As this is present in yoghurt itself you can use factory yoghurt as a starter, although this is weaker than proper culture and can result in a thinner yoghurt. This can be thickened (milk powder works well).

If you decide to make yoghurt regularly, a good investment is a cooking thermometer or, better still, an electric yoghurt-maker.

Successful yoghurt-making depends on:

(a) boiling the milk, which ensures there are no competitive bacteria left alive to vie with the bulgaris in the yoghurt.

(b) using fresh culture or yoghurt as the starter.

(c) keeping the newly mixed yoghurt warm enough to ferment and multiply for the first few hours.

(d) stopping fermentation by chilling to prevent it becoming sour.

Makes about 15oz (425g) yoghurt

1 pint (600ml) milk (not UHT)
1 tablespoon milk powder
(optional but gets thick results)

1 tablespoon bulgaris culture or
fresh yoghurt

1 Bring the milk to the boil, add the milk powder, then keep it simmering for 2–3 minutes. (Use a 4 pint/2·3 litre pan, and it won't boil over.)

2 Remove from the heat and allow to cool to just above blood temperature, about 20–30 minutes. (It should be no cooler than 104°F/40°C, no hotter than 113°F/45°C.) The age-old test in the Middle East is rather

masochistic and unhygienic – immersing the fingertips in the milk. Once you can keep them in it for 10 seconds it is ready.

3 In a mixing bowl combine the yoghurt culture or yoghurt with a few drops of the warmed milk. Mix well. Add more and more milk until it is at pouring consistency.

4 Pour this and the remaining milk into a non-metal bowl. Cover the bowl with clingfilm then put it in a warm, draught-free place to ferment (the airing cupboard or a pre-warmed switched-off oven).

5 Leave it fermenting undisturbed for at least 6 hours and no more than 8. (The longer it is left the sourer it becomes.) Put it into the fridge (to stop fermentation) for at least 2 hours.

Note: Fermentation will stop if temperature exceeds 130°F/54°C or goes below 100°F/37°C.

LABNAH

Strained Yoghurt (cheese)

Almost a staple in the Arab culinary repertoire, strained yoghurt resembles cottage or feta cheese. It is easy to make, it keeps, and is a wonderful way to use up surplus yoghurt. It is traditionally salted and stored in olive oil spiced with chilli pepper and herbs.

any quantity yoghurt
muslin or tea towel(s)

1 Over the draining board, spread out the muslin or tea towel in a sieve.

2 Put the yoghurt into the centre of it. Gather up the four corners and tie them together. Hook them over the sink tap so that the yoghurt drips into a basin. Leave for at least 10 hours.

3 Remove from the cloth and crumble and store in the fridge.

4 Or roll into small marble-sized balls and put into screw-top jar(s). Fill to the top with olive oil in which is pre-mixed salt, chilli powder (optional) and dry herbs such as tarragon. Use the fresh labnah within 3 days. The oil version, called *labnah makbous*, should be used within 10 weeks.

ABDUG OR AYRAN

Yoghurt drink

In this, yoghurt is watered down and salt or sugar is added. It is best served chilled or, better still, with crushed ice – a luxury not usually afforded to the peoples of those hot countries. It is a most refreshing and nutritious beverage, especially popular in Iran, where it is called *abdug* or just *dug*. In Armenia it is *tahn*, and elsewhere it is called *ayran* or *ayraan* or *laban* (which also means yoghurt or yoghurt drink) or *lben* in the Maghreb.

At its simplest this drink can be made with just salt or sugar, but the Iranian version is likely to include fragrant additions described as options below. It can also be made with still or aerated water.

Serves 1

$\frac{1}{3}$ *glass yoghurt*
$\frac{1}{3}$ *glass water*
$\frac{1}{3}$ *glass crushed ice*
$\frac{1}{3}$ *teaspoon aromatic salt or sugar*

$\frac{1}{3}$ *teaspoon powdered cinnamon (optional)*
$\frac{1}{3}$ *teaspoon dried mint (optional)*
$\frac{1}{3}$ *teaspoon rosewater (optional)*

1 Combine all the ingredients except the ice and beat thoroughly (electrically if you wish).

2 Put the ice into a tall tumbler and pour in the yoghurt mix over it.

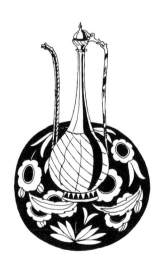

AROMATIC SALT

Throughout this book, recipes call for aromatic salt. This is salt, preferably sea salt, to which is added a light spice mixture. Ordinary salt can be used in its place, but the spicing adds a delicacy and subtlety to a recipe. It is a trick I picked up from professional chefs, and I highly recommend it.

Here are two recipes, the first being light and aromatic, the second containing spicier tastes as well as nuts. Finely grind a reasonable size batch and store in a screw-top jar.

LIGHTLY SPICED SALT

100g (4oz) coarsely granulated sea salt
1 teaspoon powdered cinnamon
1 teaspoon ground allspice

SPICIER AROMATIC SALT

1 quantity lightly spiced salt
½ teaspoon ground fenugreek seed
1 teaspoon dried mint
1 tablespoon ground almonds
½ teaspoon turmeric

YAHNI (STOCKS)

A good stock is vital for many Middle Eastern dishes. Where a recipe calls for stock, use this spicy liquid, easily made to a classic Arab recipe. If you like, use 8oz (225g) meat off-cuts and bones, adding them at stage 1. Freeze any excess for future use.

YAHNI
●

Makes 2 pints (1·1 litres)

3 pints (1·7 litres) water
1lb (450g) onions, peeled and chopped
4 cloves garlic, peeled and chopped

1 tablespoon smen
10 green cardamoms, ground
2 teaspoons ground baharat
6 bay leaves
2 teaspoons aromatic salt

1 Boil the water then add everything else.

2 Simmer for 1 hour with the lid on, by which time the stock should have reduced by half.

3 Strain and discard the solids and use as required.

TORSHI or TURSUSU or M'QALEL

Pickles

Pickles have been around for thousands of years in the Middle East. Sealed earthenware jars of *torshi* have been unearthed by archaeologists in sites as far apart as Turkey, Syria, Egypt and the Maghreb. In the olden days fruit or vegetables were pickled to last only for a few months for use over the non-growing period, and for that reason the items were often pickled unblanched. But if the pickle is to be kept for six months or more, the item should be blanched and the vinegar to water ratio stepped up to 1:1 or the water even omitted. This reduces the chance of the item going off, but it is not as crisp.

Typical pickling vegetables are turnip (*torshi lifit*), aubergine (*torshi bademjan*), carrots (*torshi jazar*), celery (*karafs*), green beans (*fasoolya*), cucumber (*khiyar*), cauliflower (*q'arnabit*), mixed vegetables (*khodar*) and green tomato (*tamaten*). Fruit pickles can include cherry (*karaz*) and peach (*kukh*).

1lb (450g) suitable vegetable or fruit (see above)
10 cloves garlic, halved

PICKLING LIQUID
1 cup distilled vinegar
2 cups water
2 tablespoons salt

1 Clean and prepare the vegetable or fruit, slice it into strips, quarters, squares as appropriate.

2 Put as much of the fruit or veg as you can into suitably sized screw-top jar(s) with the garlic cloves, dividing them between the jar(s).

3 Mix the vinegar, water and salt and pour it into the jar(s). Jiggle the jar(s) around to burst air-pockets, then top up until the jar is brim full. Store out of the sun, preferably in the dark.

4 Keep any spare pickling liquid for future use, in its own jar.

5 Examine the pickle after 48 hours to see how it is settling down. Often more liquid is needed to top it up.

6 Start eating after two weeks.

BIBER TURSU or QALI FILFIL

Vinegared chillies

I'm including this recipe by special request. Chillies are popular with many Middle Eastern heat-lovers, and vinegared chillies are especially popular in Turkey, the Levant, Yemen and the Maghreb. Factory-bottled vinegared chillies can be bought and the best of these come, in my view, from Cyprus.

So I take great pleasure in including this Cypriot recipe, not least because it is the only Cypriot recipe in the book. It is not that Cyprus does not have an interesting selection of food, but that, as with Greece, I have simply had to limit my input for space reasons. Use the small thin green or red fresh chillies, average size $3 \times \frac{1}{3}$ inch (7·5 × 1cm).

1lb (450g) hot green or red chillies
$\frac{1}{2}$ pint (300ml) distilled white
  vinegar

$\frac{1}{4}$ pint (150ml) white wine
2 teaspoons white sugar
$\frac{1}{2}$ teaspoon salt

1 Rinse and dry the chillies but do not de-stalk them.

2 Choose suitable screw-top jar(s) and cram them full of the chillies.

3 Mix the remaining ingredients together in a jug then pour it into the jars to the brim. Shake them to burst air-pockets and top up if necessary. Leave in a dark place for three or four days. Inspect and top up with spare liquid or vinegar if needed. Leave for at least four weeks before using.

LIMOON MAKBOUS

Pickled Lemon

All over the Middle East, pickled lemon is one of the highlights of the meal, its tartness contrasting well with the rich tastes of the main dishes. *Limoon makbous* can also be used to liven up cooking, particularly in Iran and the Maghreb. There are a number of variants.

TRADITIONAL METHOD

salt
4 lemons or limes, sliced
sunflower oil

1 Sprinkle two or three large dinner plates liberally with salt.

2 Put the slices on to the plates, sprinkling the tops with salt. Leave for about 24 hours, during which the salt extracts the bitterness.

3 Next day transfer the slices into suitable screw-top jar(s), carefully building up layers. When the jar is nearly full but not crammed pour in enough oil to fill the jar to the rim.

4 Leave the slices for at least a month, then start using.

ALTERNATIVE METHOD

4 lemons or limes
salt
pickling liquid (see page 42)

1 Cut each of the lemons or limes into six or eight segments. Spread them on salted plates, sprinkle with salt, and leave for at least 24 hours as in step 2 above.

2 Next day transfer the wedges into suitable screw-top jar(s), nearly filling to the top. Then pour in enough pickling liquid to fill the jar(s) to the brim.

3 Store in a dark place for three to four weeks, then begin using it.

CHAPTER 4

MEZZEH

Starters, snacks and titbits

THE mezzeh table is a Middle Eastern phenomenon. There is no equal to it anywhere else on earth – it is a gourmet's paradise. Mezzeh are small titbits of food, each on its own serving plate, from which diners make their own selection. They are served as snacks at any time of the day or night, or appetizers with drinks or the ubiquitous coffee, as hors-d'oeuvres, or as a complete meal in themselves.

A visitor to a Middle Eastern household, expected or not, must, as a matter of courtesy, be offered at least a tiny mezzeh selection, even if it is no more than olives, cheese or dates.

There must be a number of dishes to make mezzeh and the more the better: invention and ingenuity are the keys to success. Most of us in the West have encountered mezzeh at our local Greek, Turkish or Lebanese restaurant, where they are served as starters. Very pleasant (and often very filling) they are, but the range is always limited to a few trusted favourites of perhaps half a dozen choices. In the Middle East, it is a matter of pride as to how many are prepared. Mezzeh do not appear with every meal, but when they do the average cook at home may aim at eight or ten choices, and if entertaining, perhaps twenty. A restaurant should certainly average forty to fifty. A prestige establishment or a celebration party – a wedding or a birthday – could muster up as much as four times more.

The word mezzeh is probably derived from the Greek word *maza*, meaning mixture. In Tunisia mezzeh are called *aadou* whilst in Algeria they are *kemia*.

Some mezzeh are simple to prepare – nuts, olives, cheeses, raw vegetables and fruit, for example. Salads of invariable combinations are mandatory, and cold puréed dips inevitably appear, the best known of which are *houmous b'tahine* and taramasalata. Hot soups thick and thin are popular. Stir-fried and deep-fried items give the mezzeh selection zest and interest, and can be brought to the table sizzling hot as and when.

The recipes in this chapter are a good cross-section of mezzeh items, but you can also add items from the other chapters in this book. Always serve one or more types of Middle Eastern bread as accompaniment.

Houmous B'Tahine

Chickpea and sesame dip

Probably the best-known Middle Eastern dish, this is a purée made from chickpeas (houmous) and sesame seed paste (tahine). It is a dip, and its texture can range from quite coarse and porridge-like to very fine. You can determine the texture of your choice by the amount of grinding. Traditionally it is hand-ground with a mortar and pestle, while a food processor does it in seconds. A blender will require added water, so will result in a runnier texture. This recipe freezes well and I like to make a large batch (treble this recipe) to save kitchen mess. Adjust the garlic, lemon and oil quantities to suit your palate. Olive oil is traditional, but its powerful flavour is not to everyone's taste. Try hazelnut oil for a truly delicious variation.

Serves 4 generously

5oz (150g) whole, dry chickpeas
3 tablespoons tahine paste
1–4 cloves garlic
1–3 tablespoons lemon juice

1–3 tablespoons olive or hazelnut oil
salt to taste

1 Pick through the chickpeas, removing discoloured ones and pieces of grit etc. Then rinse them and place them in a 3 pint (1·75 litre) saucepan or bowl with 2 pints (1·1 litres) of cold water. Leave them to soak for at least 12 hours during which time they will swell in size.

2 Boil about 2 pints (1·1 litres) of water. Strain then rinse the chickpeas. Put them in the boiling water and simmer for about 45 minutes.

3 Check they are soft, then strain and run under cold water (or set aside to cool). You can freeze whole cooked chickpeas at this stage.

4 If using a food processor simply place the chickpeas, with the other ingredients, in it and whizz away. The longer you run it the finer the texture. Add a little water to assist the processor as required. If using a blender, you will need more water. Grinding by hand is slow. Start with the peas first, adding the remaining ingredients as you achieve your purée.

5 Chill in the fridge for at least 30 minutes for best results. Serve with hot Arab bread and a salad.

QUICK HOUMOUS B'TAHINE

Serves 4 generously

1 × 14oz (400g) can cooked
  chickpeas
3 tablespoons tahine paste
$\frac{1}{2}$–2 teaspoons garlic powder

1 tablespoon lemon juice
2 tablespoons olive or hazelnut oil
salt to taste

1   Strain the contents of the can. Grind the chickpeas to the texture of your choice, using as much of the liquid from the can as you need.

2   Mix in the remaining ingredients. Serve chilled.

TARAMASALATA

Salted fish roe dip

Equally well known in the West is this creamy pink-coloured dip. Originating in ancient Greece, it is to be found in Turkey, the Caucasian countries, and with slight variations throughout the Levant and the Gulf. The key to both taste and colour is the fish roe from mullet (*tarama*). This lobster-coloured roe is salted and dried or available bottled or canned. If you can obtain *tarama* you will be sure of the authentic taste, but a close substitute is smoked cod's roe. The bright rose pink taramasalata of the Western delicatessen is often 'enhanced' with red food colouring. Yesterday's pitta bread is always used in taramasalata to 'soften' the flavour and to bulk out the purée. You can substitute British bread, white or brown, the latter giving a better taste and colour than white, in my view. This dish can be made in larger quantities (treble the recipe) and frozen in portions.

Serves 4 generously

1 pitta bread or 2 slices white or
  brown bread, crusts removed
$3\frac{1}{2}$oz (100g) salted tarama or
  smoked cod's roe
1–4 cloves garlic, chopped
1–3 tablespoons lemon juice
1–3 tablespoons olive oil
$\frac{1}{8}$ teaspoon red food colouring
  (optional)

GARNISH
sprig of parsley, fennel or
  coriander
a sprinkling of paprika
1 black olive

1 Grind the pitta or bread into soft 'crumbs'.

2 Add the remaining ingredients and pulse them in the machine until they are mixed together. Add a little water to achieve the purée texture of your choice.

3 Garnish, and serve chilled with hot pitta bread and a salad.

QUICK TARAMASALATA

Serves 4 generously

$3\frac{1}{2}$oz (100g) roe as above, or
  smoked salmon
$3\frac{1}{2}$oz (100g) thick Greek yoghurt or
  cream cheese

$\frac{1}{2}$–2 teaspoons garlic powder
1–3 tablespoons lemon juice
1–3 tablespoons olive oil

Pulse down in a food processor/blender. Serve as above.

SABRA DIP

Avocado dip

Sabra is an Israeli colloquialism for those people born in the new Israel. It is also a desert cactus. Avocados are relatively new to Israel, having been first planted in Palestine by Jewish settlers early this century. They are now a major Israeli export.

Dips are as old as the Middle East itself, forming an important part of the mezzeh table. This fine new Israeli recipe is ideal as a starter served with 'dip sticks' such as celery, cucumber, carrot strips, raw mushrooms, potato crisps, etc, and with hot pitta bread. It can also be an accompaniment to the main course.

Serves 4

1 ripe avocado
½ green capsicum pepper
4oz (110g) onion
3 tablespoons lemon juice

6oz (175g) cottage or cream
   cheese, or soured cream or
   strained (Greek) yoghurt or a
   combination
milk as required
salt to taste

1 Halve the avocado, remove the stone and scoop out the flesh. If using an electric food processor or liquidizer, coarsely chop the flesh of the avocado, pepper and onion, and put into the machine with the remaining ingredients. If doing it by hand, mash the avocado, finely chop the pepper and onion, then fold in the remaining ingredients.

2 Use the milk to obtain the thickness of texture you require and add salt to taste. Chill in the fridge for an hour or so before serving. The lemon juice minimizes discoloration, but if the dip develops a dark skin on top, carefully scrape this off before serving.

HILBEH or HULBA

Hot fenugreek dip

This dip originated in the deep south of the Arabian Gulf. There are many variations: the Yemeni version, for instance, is very chilli hot, and the paste is spread on *khoubz* (bread) before it is baked. With or without chilli, this dip is very spicy and rather an acquired taste, for fenugreek is bitter. I have considerably reduced the fenugreek level in this recipe, but even so it is not for the faint-hearted. Soaking the seeds until they soften and swell, with a jelly-like coating, removes some of the bitterness. Use as a dip or as an accompaniment to a main-course dish.

Sufficient for several servings

2 tablespoons fenugreek seeds
4 tablespoons vegetable or olive
 oil
4–8 cloves garlic, chopped
4oz (110g) onion, chopped
1 teaspoon ground baharat (see page 33)

2oz (50g) fresh coriander leaves,
 chopped (about $\frac{1}{2}$ bunch)
3–4 canned plum tomatoes
3 tablespoons lemon juice
2–6 fresh green chillies, de-stalked
 and chopped

1 Pick through the fenugreek seeds, removing grit etc. Put them in a bowl with $\frac{1}{4}$ pint (150ml) water, and leave for at least 12 hours or overnight.

2 Heat the oil, and fry the garlic for 1 minute. Add the onion and fry that for 3 minutes, stirring frequently. Strain the fenugreek seeds then add them to the frying pan, stirring for 3 more minutes. Add the *baharat* and the fresh coriander. Stir-fry for another 3 minutes then allow to cool.

3 Put the remaining ingredients into a food processor or blender and pulse into a purée.

4 Add the cooled fried mixture and continue pulsing to obtain a thickish purée.

HARISSA

Hot red chilli purée

Harissa is a spiced chilli sauce which accompanies dishes in the North African countries. This particular recipe comes from Tunisia, where they like their food particularly hot. (The Algerian version is called *dersa*, and the Moroccan *felfel sudani*.) The texture should be fine but thick, and the colour deep red, rather like tomato sauce or ketchup. Fresh red chillies should be used for the colour, and to get the fine texture, the chillies and tomatoes should be de-seeded. This sauce should be extremely hot, and those who adore heat should add the chilli powder and omit the red capsicum peppers.

Harissa is available canned, but it is easy to make. It will keep in the fridge for several days, and it freezes well. A good idea, if you adore hot accompaniments, is to make a large batch – say double or treble the amount below – then freeze it in a number of yoghurt pots.

Sufficient for several servings

20 *fresh red chillies,*
   or 5 fresh red chillies and 2 red
   capsicum peppers
4 *canned plum tomatoes*
2 *cloves garlic, chopped*

1 *teaspoon ground cummin*
1 *teaspoon ground coriander*
1–4 *teaspoons very hot chilli*
   powder (optional)
vinegar (any kind)

1 De-stalk, slit and de-seed the chillies and the red peppers if used. De-seed the tomatoes.

2 Put everything, except the vinegar, into a food processor or blender and give it a good long run (of about 3 minutes) to get a very fine texture. Add just enough vinegar during the run to ensure it turns into a stiffish paste.

3 If you have no electrical tools, the old-fashioned way is to use a pestle and mortar and grind it all to a purée.

TARATOOR B'SADE

Garlic dip

Middle Easterners adore garlic, as an encounter with any friendly Arab will prove. Rather than wince as ferociously flavoured breath wafts over you, get stuck in on the 'if you can't beat 'em join 'em' principle. But what is done over 'there' needs rather more thought over 'here', as this dish is totally uncompromising. It is pure raw garlic. So if you have someone to impress or flatter over the next day or two, do not eat this dip.

The smelliest part is the preparation and washing up, so I advise making a largish batch and freezing it in batches in yoghurt pots. To avoid tainting everything else in the freezer, after breaking the dip out of the yoghurt pot mould, wrap each block in a plastic bag and seal it. Put all the bags in a large bag and seal it and put the bag into a plastic lidded box.

Enough for many servings

30–40 cloves garlic, skinned and chopped
6 tablespoons olive oil

3 tablespoons lemon juice
salt to taste

Put everything into the food processor or blender. Use a little water to obtain the purée texture you require.

DUKKAH

Crumbly spicy nut dip

Dukkah is the name given to any dry mixture of spices, herbs and nuts, etc. Also called *do'ah* and *za'tar*, these mixtures are sold by street traders in twists of newspaper to eat there and then as an appetizer or to add as a condiment to a main dish. Variants are found all over the Middle East.

This *dukkah* is from Egypt, and it is eaten with *aish* (Egyptian bread), first dunked in olive oil and then into the *dukkah* bowl. The dish has existed in Egypt since the times of the pharaohs, and was consumed by slaves and rulers alike. *Dukkah* was undoubtedly supplied in the pyramids to sustain their occupants on the long journey to the hereafter, and has survived into contemporary times as a poor man's meal. Today it is likely to appear as one of many dishes on the mezzeh table.

The important thing to remember about *dukkah* is that it should be dry and crumbly. It is easy to over-grind the ingredients, especially the nuts, and make the mixture hot and oily. To prevent this, cool the ingredients after roasting, then proceed *slowly*.

Enough for several servings

5oz (150g) hazelnuts, shelled
2oz (50g) sesame seeds
1 teaspoon coriander seeds
2 teaspoons cummin seeds

$\frac{1}{2}$ teaspoon aromatic salt
1 teaspoon za'atar spice mix
12–15 fresh mint leaves, chopped

1 Pre-heat oven to 325°F/160°C/Gas 3, then put the nuts and seeds on to an oven tray and into the oven for exactly 10 minutes. Remove and cool down completely.

2 When cold put into the food processor (a blender doesn't work as well) with the other ingredients and pulse until the mixture is crumbly. Pause between pulses to prevent overheating and therefore oiling up.

3 Serve as described above, or use as a condiment sprinkled over other dishes. The mixture will keep in an airtight container for several weeks. It does become stale after that time, but if you're left with some, you can cook it into a Middle Eastern vegetable or meat dish to use it up.

TA'LEYAH or TAQLIYA

Fried garlic and onion garnish

Originating in ancient Egypt, this simple garnish is used to liven up vegetable dishes such as *melokhia* and *ful nabed*, which might otherwise be slightly bland. It can, of course, be used to garnish any dish of your choice.

Serves 4

4 cloves garlic
8oz (225g) onion
4 tablespoons olive oil

1 Cut the garlic cloves into long thin strips, and do the same with the onion, cross-cutting the strips so that they are approximately the same size as the garlic.

2 Heat the olive oil to smoking.

3 Put the garlic and onion into the oil and briskly stir-fry for 1 minute, then continue to stir-fry for 5 more minutes. The mixture should be well browned and crispy. Serve hot as a garnish.

MUTABBEL (BABA GANOVJ)

Aubergine and tahine dip

The aubergine is greatly relished all over the Middle East, and because it is very soft in texture, it works really well as a purée. The dish is particularly popular in the Levant, where it is also called *baba ganovj*, and is often to be found in Lebanese restaurants in the West. Variations will be found in Turkey, the Gulf (in Arabic *mutabbel* means spiced), and Iran (where they add ground dried fruit and yoghurt to the purée). The dish should have an intriguing smoky taste, and this is obtained by baking the aubergine over charcoal until the outside skin is quite burnt. Then the pulp is scraped out and the skin discarded. Try this the next time you barbecue. The alternative is to grill it at low heat until it burns (turning it two or three times).

Serves 4

12oz (350g) aubergine
1–4 cloves garlic, chopped
2 tablespoons tahine paste
2–4 tablespoons Greek yoghurt
  (optional)
2 or 3 pieces dried apricot
  (optional)

1 tablespoon lemon juice
salt to taste
a pinch of chilli powder (optional)
a sprig of parsley, chopped

1 Wash the aubergine but leave the stalk on. Prick it a few times with the tip of a knife.

2 Bake it over charcoal, or under a low to medium-heat grill with the rack at lowest level, or in an oven pre-heated to 325°F/160°C/Gas 3. Cook until the skin has blistered and is charred. Times will vary, but it will take more than 20 minutes. Inspect regularly.

3 Remove from the heat, halve whilst hot, and scoop out all the flesh, discarding the skin.

4 Place the aubergine flesh, garlic, tahine, and yoghurt and apricot (if wanted) into the food processor/blender, and pulse to a soft texture (or mash by hand). Add the lemon juice and salt to taste.

5 Serve cold, garnishing with the chilli powder and chopped parsley.

TABOULEH

Mixed salad with burghul (cracked wheat)

Tabouleh is a very ancient dish. Originally it consisted largely of burghul accompanied by mixed herbs, and it was a substantial 'peasant' meal. Modern recipes usually reverse the balance and the burghul quantity is minimal. This recipe uses about 25 per cent burghul and the remainder salad vegetables of your choice. The burghul quantity can be increased or decreased to taste.

Provided that you are using burghul (which is pre-cooked, cracked and dried), no further cooking is required. Ordinary cracked wheat will require brief boiling. There are two ways of using burghul for this dish, which I detail below. Tabouleh is a must as a mezzeh, starter or side dish. One attractive serving variation is to put the tabouleh into 'cups' of lettuce or vine leaves.

Serves 4

$3\frac{1}{2}$oz (100g) burghul (cracked processed wheat)
1 iceberg lettuce
10–15 cherry tomatoes
1 bunch spring onions
1–2 bunches parsley
$\frac{1}{2}$ bunch coriander leaves

20–30 mint leaves
4 tablespoons olive oil
3 tablespoons fresh lemon juice
$\frac{1}{2}$ teaspoon freshly milled black pepper
$\frac{1}{2}$ teaspoon baharat
aromatic salt to taste

1 If you want the burghul to have a soft texture soak it in 1 pint (570ml) cold water for 20 minutes then strain it; squeeze out all the excess water then set aside whilst you prepare the salad. If you want it to be crunchy add it dry to stage 4.

2 Wash and chop the salad vegetables and herbs, then chop and toss in a large bowl.

3 Whisk the olive oil and lemon juice with a fork and toss into the salad.

4 Add the burghul, pepper, *baharat* and salt. Toss once more and set aside (preferably in the fridge) for half an hour or so to allow the flavours to blend.

FATTOUSH

Mixed salad with toasted bread

Arab bread, *khoubiz* or pitta, is delicious hot and fresh, but left until next day it goes hard and unappetizing. This salad from ancient times incorporated a resourceful way of using old bread up. *Fattoush* literally means 'wet bread' and traditionally the *khoubiz* was soaked in water then slit along the edge into two discs, then it was toasted so that it became crisp. This recipe omits the soaking and you can use fresh or frozen and thawed Arab bread.

The salad vegetables here are suggestions – use any of your choice, but I do recommend the spinach, which is unusual. It can be substituted for *melokhia* (Egyptian) or *rijlah* (Arab) leaves; these are virtually unobtainable in the West and are mandatory in a real *fattoush*.

Serves 4

2 pieces khoubiz or pitta bread
1 head Chinese leaves or 1 iceberg
  lettuce
4–6 spinach leaves
4 inch (10cm) piece cucumber
4oz (110g) onion
1 bunch parsley
10–15 fresh mint leaves

2 cloves garlic, finely chopped
  (optional)
4 tablespoons olive oil
3 tablespoons fresh lemon juice
$\frac{1}{2}$ teaspoon freshly milled black
  pepper
aromatic salt to taste

1 Slit open the bread along its edge to make two discs, then grill at low heat until crisp and golden. Or bake the bread in the oven (while being used for something else) at 325°F/160°C/Gas 3 for 10–15 minutes. Allow to cool then cut into pieces about $\frac{1}{2}$ inch (1cm) square.

2 Wash and chop the salad vegetables and herbs, and toss in a large bowl.

3 Whisk the olive oil and lemon juice with a fork and toss into the salad. Put the salad aside (preferably in the fridge) for half an hour or so.

4 Just before serving toss in the pepper, aromatic salt and the bread pieces.

LOUB'YEH B'ZAYT

Green bean salad in olive oil

You won't travel far in the Middle East without encountering this delicious salad. Sometimes tomatoes are included, sometimes not, so I have made them optional. The beans normally used are thin string or runner beans, but Kenyan beans are perfect. The dish is cooked and can be served hot, although it is usually served lukewarm. I also like it cold. Eat with hot *khoubiz* bread.

Serves 4

12oz (350g) French (Kenyan) or
  small runner beans
4 tablespoons olive oil
2–4 cloves garlic (optional)
4oz (110g) onion, chopped
4–6 canned plum tomatoes,
  chopped (optional)

1 teaspoon chilli powder
  (optional)
½ teaspoon freshly milled black
  pepper
aromatic salt
1 tablespoon freshly chopped
  coriander

1 Top, tail and wash the beans, stringing them if necessary. Cut into 2 inch (5cm) pieces.

2 Put them into 2 pints (1·2 litres) boiling water, and simmer for 5 minutes.

3 Meanwhile heat the olive oil, and stir-fry the garlic and onion for 3 minutes. Add the tomatoes and chilli powder, if using. Stir-fry for a minute, mashing the tomatoes.

4 Add the (strained) beans and simmer for 5 minutes. Stir in the pepper, salt and fresh coriander.

SABZI ISFAHAN KHODRAN

Mixed herbal salad

A delightful tradition at the Iranian dining table is the appearance before anything else of a large ornamental dish containing a mixture of as many varieties of fresh herbs that the host can obtain. In Iran this will certainly include herbs that we have never heard of over here – some bitter, some sweet, all fragrant and tasty. Huge hot pieces of floppy *nane lavash* (bread) and yoghurt or *samneh* are also served, and the diner scoops up the herbs and a little yoghurt or *samneh* in a piece of bread, and has as healthy and enticing an appetizer as can be conceived. The bowl stays on the table throughout the meal, enabling the diners to garnish other dishes to their liking. It is a splendid idea and you can let your imagination run riot with ingredients, especially if you are lucky enough to have a herb garden.

My combination varies depending on availability, but usually contains all of the first seven ingredients and one or two of the last four. Note that there is no dressing or seasoning. These would overwhelm the subtlety of the herbs. Use any spare to make vegetable stock.

Plenty for 4

1 head chicory	30 mint leaves
1 head endive	1 punnet mustard and cress
1 bunch parsley	sprigs of fresh herbs, such as dill,
1 bunch chives	basil, fennel and marjoram
1 bunch watercress	

1 Wash, shake dry, de-stalk and discard unwanted bits as necessary.

2 Chop to your liking and toss in a large bowl.

3 For best (crispiest) results, cover the bowl and put it in the fridge for a minimum of 2 hours (and a maximum of 4).

SHORBA BIL HOUT

Fish soup

This is one of the few Libyan recipes in this book, although variations of it, mainly differing in the spice content, will be found as far apart as Morocco and the Gulf. Soups such as this one are bubbling and ready to serve the moment the sun sets to break the day-long fast during Ramadan.

In the Middle East, a soup is unlikely to be served as a starter. It is more likely to appear as the main-course dish and with relishes. As such it will be less liquid than a conventional soup, and you can make this dish into a main course by using less water. My personal preference is for smoked haddock – I like its colour and salty taste – but you can use plaice, cod, white haddock or indeed any fish of preference. Serve piping hot.

Serves 4 as a soup, 2 as a main-course dish

12oz (350g) smoked haddock, weighed after step 1 (2 fleshy fish should be enough)	1 recipe chermoula (see page 34) 4 canned plum tomatoes, chopped 4 sprigs parsley
1½ pints (900ml) water	

1 Skin, bone and cut the haddock up into chunky pieces averaging 2 inches (5cm) in length.

2 Boil the water, add the fish, *chermoula* and tomatoes, and simmer for 20 minutes. (The dish can be puréed at this stage, a preference in many Middle Eastern households.)

3 Serve in soup bowls, garnishing with parsley.

4 As a main-course dish, halve the water content. Stir during the cooking.

MANTIQ MEHAMMER

Fried squid

A few years ago I was working on a contract in Tunisia. The job involved the importation of some equipment to the small island of Jerba. This involved a cast, it seemed, of dozens of Tunisian officials – customs, police, agents, taxmen, you name it – and tons of paperwork. The only highlights amid days of tedium in dusty down-town Houmt Souk, were frequent visits to a tiny market-place café. It had no name and no menu. It just served the best Tunisian dishes you could find. This simple squid dish was one of them.

Serves 4 as a starter

12oz (350g) squid
4 tablespoons olive oil
4–6 cloves garlic, finely chopped
2oz (50g) onion, finely chopped

2 fresh green chillies, finely chopped
1 teaspoon turmeric
2 teaspoons dried mint

1 Wash and clean the squid removing any unwanted membranes etc. Then cut into rings.

2 Heat the oil then stir-fry the remaining ingredients for 2 or 3 minutes. Add the squid and stir-fry for about 15 minutes. To prevent it sticking, add a little water from time to time.

3 Serve sizzling hot with a side salad, lemon wedges, *harissa* (chilli sauce) and *khoubiz* bread.

HARIRA MDIQ

Lamb and lentil soup

Harira is a thick-textured Moroccan soup – a gruel really – of which there are literally unlimited variations. It was originally a Berber hill people's dish. It still is simple, but you can have this dish as a house speciality in 5-star hotels (at enormous expense) or at market food stalls (for pennies). It is eaten at breakfast and last thing at night and at all times in between. It also figures largely during the month of Ramadan. I was fortunate enough to obtain this recipe from a Berber who spent his summers as a life-guard at a holiday hotel in the town of Mdiq in Mediterranean Morocco. Each winter he would exchange his jeans and Walkman for his Rif mountain home town and his striped Berber robes. (Mdiq, by the way, is pronounced Mideek by Europeans and something gutteral and inimitable by the locals, sounding like a cough and a spit.)

Serves 4

6oz (175g) red lentils
4oz (110g) lean lamb, cut into ½ inch (1cm) cubes
8oz (225g) onion, chopped
1 tablespoon la kama spice mix
6 tomatoes, skinned and chopped
1 red capsicum pepper, chopped

2 fresh green chillies, chopped (optional)
2 tablespoons freshly chopped coriander
25–30 saffron strands
salt

1 Pick through the lentils to remove grit etc, rinse, then soak them in 2 pints (1·2 litres) cold water for 1 hour. Then strain.

2 Boil up 2 pints (1·2 litres) water. Put the lentils, lamb and onion into the pan and simmer for about half an hour. Stir from time to time.

3 Add the *la kama*, tomatoes, capsicum and optional chillies and simmer for 20 more minutes.

4 Add the fresh coriander, saffron and salt to taste. Simmer for 3 or 4 more minutes then serve piping hot.

FELAFEL AND TA'AMIAH

Ground chickpea croquettes

Both Israel and Egypt claim felafel as their own national dish. Historically the honours probably go to Egypt, where it is called *ta'amiah*. The Egyptian version is made from ground *ful nabed* (white broad beans) and is rissole shaped, whereas Israeli felafels are made from ground chickpeas and are spherical. There is plentiful evidence to show that they existed in Pharaonic times when the Jews were the slaves of Egypt. But felafels have survived in both cultures for 3,000 years and that alone is remarkable.

Once you have tasted the real thing you are hooked, but some factory-produced mixes now available are disappointing. Felafels are easy to make yourself. They take a bit of time, but they taste really good, so it is worth the effort (I make a large batch and freeze the spares). Serve hot with salad, *khoubiz* bread and *houmous b'tahine*.

Serves 4

1lb 2oz (500g) dry chickpeas
½oz (15g) fresh yeast (optional)
2–4 cloves garlic, chopped
4oz (110g) onion, roughly chopped
1 teaspoon ground cummin
1 teaspoon ground coriander
1 tablespoon freshly chopped coriander

1 tablespoon tahine paste
1 tablespoon lemon juice
1 teaspoon aromatic salt

TO COOK
dry breadcrumbs
oil for deep-frying

1 Pick through the chickpeas to remove grit etc. Rinse them, then put them into a pan large enough to hold 3 pints (1·75 litres) cold water and the chickpeas, and allow them to swell. Leave for at least 12 hours or overnight.

2 Strain, rinse then grind the chickpeas to an even, coarse texture. You can use a mincer or food processor.

3 The yeast will partly leaven the mixture, creating lighter felafels, but it can be omitted. Stir the yeast into 3 tablespoons of warm water, then, when dissolved, add it and all the remaining felafel ingredients to the ground chickpeas. Grind into a mouldable paste, adding enough water to achieve this.

4 Knead the mixture like dough, then leave it to stand in a warm place for 30 minutes or so to allow the yeast to take effect and the flavours to blend.

5 Re-knead the mixture.

6 To get the precise number of felafels you require of equal size, I find it easier to divide the mixture into quarters, then to sub-divide each quarter into six (if you want a total of twenty-four felafels) or four (if you want sixteen larger ones). Alternatively use a melon baller to obtain equal size and shape.

7 Sprinkle breadcrumbs on the work surface and gently roll each felafel into a sphere. When they are all made let them stand again in a warmish place for 15–20 minutes, during which time you can heat up your deep-frying oil to 375°F/190°C (chip-frying temperature).

8 Then one at a time, place eight felafels into the oil and fry until golden brown. I find 10 minutes is enough, but the timing depends on the size of the felafel so keep your eye on them after 5 or 6 minutes.

9 Remove from the oil and rest on kitchen paper in a warm place until you are ready to serve them all. Alternatively, they will re-heat in an oven and they will freeze.

TA'AMIAH VARIATION

In place of the chickpeas use the same weight of dry white (skinless) broad beans (*ful nabed*). The remaining ingredients and preparation are the same: but instead of spheres make rissole-shaped discs; and instead of breadcrumbs, press the discs into sesame seeds.

MERGUEZ

Spiced mutton sausages

The British sausage is a small cylindrical casing containing spiceless ground raw meat (usually pork), which, when cooked, is transformed into a tasty crisp favourite. The people of the Mediterranean have a totally different perception of the sausage. Their's is of a combination of chopped or ground meat (often beef or mutton), which is encased with spices, in intestines traditionally, and hung to dry in the sun.

The origin of the sausage seems to lie with ancient Mediterranean mariners whose meat supply had to be safely preserved and conveniently packaged. The Phoenicians, the great sea traders of the first millennium BC, whose bases were dotted all around the Med, probably introduced the concept to Spain, Italy, Armenia and Tunisia. In those countries today we find sausages bearing much similarity: in Spain the *chorizo*, in Italy the *mortadella* and *salami*, in Armenia the *gologig*, and in Tunisia and the Maghreb, the *merguez*. They are eaten as appetizers or used to flavour cooking. These days it is quite normal to find all or some of these items in good delicatessens.

It isn't practical to produce them exactly at home without detailed curing and long sun-drying, but this recipe for *merguez* produces a cooked sausage which can subsequently be frozen for further use. The only special ingredient is the casing. You can use edible artificial casings also available from butchers. This recipe makes 12 *merguez* (making any less is hardly worth the effort) and you can freeze the spares.

Makes 12 sausages, enough for several servings

1½lb (675g) lean mutton, lamb or
  beef
6–8 cloves garlic, crushed
1 tablespoon finely ground ras-el-
  hanout

6 tablespoons olive oil
2 teaspoons sea salt
4½ feet (1·5m) sausage casing

1 The meat is best coarsely minced, so use a hand or electric mincer.

2 Add the other ingredients and mix throughly by hand. Put the mixture into a piping bag with a large nozzle.

3 Clean your hands, then tie the bottom of the casing into a knot. Cut the casing to about 1½ feet (45cm) in length, and put the open end securely over the piping nozzle. Squeeze the mixture into the casing, pushing it along to the knotted end, but do not *over* fill. When evenly distributed, and one-third of the mixture is used, disengage the sausage and tie off the open end.

4 Now create three 1 inch (2·5cm) gaps in the casing to create four sausages 4 inches (10cm) each. Gently spin the casing at each gap and tie it with cotton (I find trying to knot the casing usually splits it open). Re-squeeze the meat back up to each knot.

5 Repeat steps 3 and 4 twice more, to make twelve sausages.

6 *Merguez* are traditionally boiled or grilled over charcoal. I prefer to oven roast them – they stay intact that way.

7 Pre-heat oven to 275°F/140°C/Gas 1. Fit the sausages on a couple of oven trays, allowing them plenty of space, and roast for 20 minutes. Inspect and turn them, then up the temperature to 350°F/180°C/Gas 4, giving them a further 20–30 minutes. Inspect again half way, turning as necessary to prevent sticking and uneven cooking.

8 Serve hot or cold or use to flavour other dishes such as *couscous* meat stew or *chakchouka*.

KIBID MILI

Sautéed liver

Really, what could be simpler than this? Strips of liver, coated with a mixture of flour and spices, and fried in oil. Every country mentioned in this book has one or more recipes for this dish, under a wealth of different titles. In Turkey, for example, there is *ciger tavasi*; in Qatar there is *kibda bi tum*, which uses garlic a-plenty, in Egypt they have a variation using goose liver, *kibda ma'liya*. In Libya they roll the liver in partially crushed cummin seeds and it is called *kabda camman*.

The liver can be from lamb, sheep, calf, goose, chicken or (but not for Jews and Moslems) pig. The cut can vary from whole livers to delicate strips. Above all the spicing of this dish varies from mere salt and pepper in Armenia to explosive in Tunisia and the Yemen. The Iraqi recipe here is spiced to medium level.

Serves 4

12oz (350g) liver (see above)
5oz (150g) plain flour
1–2 tablespoons baharat

6–8 tablespoons sesame oil
4 lemon wedges
sprigs of parsley or other herbs

1 Wash the liver, remove all unpleasantries, then cut into strips averaging $\frac{1}{2} \times 3$ inches (1 × 7·5cm).

2 Mix the flour and *baharat* and put on a wide plate, near the stove.

3 Heat the oil in a pan (I use a wok because it is best for stir-frying).

4 Coat the first few liver pieces in the flour mixture and drop them straight into the wok. Stir-fry, then coat the next few pieces and build up a pan-full in this way until half the pieces are in. This keeps the oil temperature up and prevents the flour becoming soggy.

5 Fry for 5 minutes or so, moving the strips around so that they all cook evenly. Remove and strain.

6 Repeat stages 4 and 5 with the remaining liver pieces.

7 Serve sizzling with a lemon wedge and herb garnish.

RIGHT, CLOCKWISE FROM THE TOP: *Taramasalata* page 47, *Mantiq Mehammer* (fried squid) page 59, *Houmous B'Tahine* (chickpea and sesame dip) page 46, *Sabra Dip* (avocado dip) page 49, *Tabouleh* (mixed salad with burghul) page 55, *Harissa* (chilli purée) page 51, *Pitta*, page 154.

MIDYE IZMIRI TAVASI

Batter-coated mussels

The city of Izmir is in western Turkey, and nestles amidst the islands and river mouths of the Aegean Sea, a truly beautiful part of the world. It is also very ancient, for Izmir was founded over 2,000 years ago. It was then called Smyrna and was an important trading city during ancient Greek, Byzantine and Ottoman times. Nowhere in the world is there better seafood than in this part of the Aegean, and this recipe, said to date back to those times, is from the excellent Buyuk Efes Oteli, Izmir's top hotel.

You'll find this dish all over Turkey using different varieties of mussels. I have used the largish orangey pink ones with dark blue-black shells, sold in Britain by the pint. This generally gives between 32 and 40 fresh mussels with shell on, which is around 1lb (450g). To control your portions ask the fishmonger for the exact number you want (but allow a few extras in case some are duds).

Serves 4 as a starter

40 *fresh mussels*	2oz (50g) *cornflour*
BATTER	1 *egg*
3oz (75g) *plain white flour*	1 *teaspoon aromatic salt*
	milk

1 In a deep bowl, mix the flours, egg, salt and enough milk to make a batter the consistency of ketchup. Stand for 20 minutes to blend.

2 Meanwhile prepare the mussels. Choose only those which are tightly closed. Scrub well and remove beards. Put in a pan with a little water and heat for a few minutes until they open. Remove from the shells. Discard any still closed.

3 Heat the oil to 375°F/190°C (chip-frying temperature).

4 Immerse one mussel at a time into the batter and drop it into the hot oil. Put no more than ten at once into the frier (this keeps the temperature up and the result crisper). Fry for about 4 minutes then remove, drain on kitchen paper and keep warm. Repeat until all the mussels are cooked.

5 Serve on a bed of lettuce or radiccio with a lemon wedge.

LEFT, CLOCKWISE FROM THE TOP: *Bisteeya* (pigeon pie) page 72, *Spanokopitta* (spinach with feta cheese pie) page 74, with its filling in the small bowl below, *Pastelles* (puff pastry pot) page 76, with mince and rice fillings below, *Boreks* (small stuffed pastries) page 67, *S'finah* (tiny Arab pizzas with quail's eggs) page 77, and above them seafood and vegetable fillings.

CHAPTER · 5

PASTRY ITEMS

IF THE peoples of the Middle East are united about anything it is their love of pastry. It appears at most meals and in many forms, perhaps the most celebrated of which is filo pastry, that amazing thin pastry developed in ancient Greece. It appears in pastry recipes of all sorts, the most popular of which is undoubtedly the Turkish inspired *borek*. Almost every Middle Eastern country now has its range of *borek*-style finger pastries of various shapes and sizes with a wide range of fillings, and they are all delicious. Equally well known and ubiquitous are the two filo pastry sweetmeats, baklava and *kadaif*: the former is a sandwich of crunchy filo sheets interleaved with crushed nuts and dripping honey and syrup; the latter a shredded filo version. Other uses of filo include larger pastry dishes, among them *bisteeya* (a Moroccan speciality, pigeon pie) and *spanakopitta* (spinach and cheese pie from Greece, the heartland of filo) with its derivatives *tyropitta* (egg and cheese) and *kotopitta* (chicken).

Although filo is the star performer of the Middle Eastern pastry department, it by no means has a solo role. Ordinary puff or short pastry also have their places in such recipes as the *pastele*, a lidded round puff pastry pot from Israel. A rather surprising recipe which I could not fail to give you is the Arabian pizza, *lahma-bi-ajeen*. Originating in the Gulf, this is a flat disc of pastry on which is baked a delicious savoury topping.

The dishes in this chapter are just a representative selection of pastries from the Middle East, covering as wide a variety of styles as possible.

FILO AND WARKAH

All over the Middle East, from Morocco to Saudi, to Turkey and Greece, there is a tradition of making pastries with a dough which is literally as thin yet as strong as tracing paper. The methods of making this varies quite markedly. Best known to us is the Greek filo pastry, called *yufka* in Turkey. It is also the pastry used to make strudels. The dough for filo pastry is straightforward enough, being a mixture of flour, water and oil.

66

A modest lump, the size of a tennis ball, is kneaded until it is very elastic, then it is rolled and stretched until it is thin and translucent (the name comes from the Greek for 'leaf'). Commercially, it is rolled to a sheet about 4 feet (1·25 metres) square: this is slightly hardened then cut into sheets, usually 20 × 12 inches (50 × 30 cm), and sealed in packs of twelve (250 g) or twenty-four (500 g). It takes professionals some years to master the skills required to make filo, and it is very difficult to make at home, requiring a special long thin rolling pin, extreme patience and plentiful practice. Factory-made sheets are excellent, however, and can be obtained fresh or frozen from good delicatessens. Chinese spring roll pastry can also be used.

The Maghreb has developed its own method of making translucent thin pastry. The Moroccan *warkah* or *ouarkah* (called *dioul* in Algeria and *madsouka* in Tunisia) is made by dabbing a wettish lump of dough on a hot griddle pan to create a 3 inch (7·5 cm) disc. This operation is repeated with overlapping dabs, perhaps forty or fifty times, until a disc some 18 inches (45 cm) is created. This is lifted off the pan and the operation starts again. A 'professional' can create a stack of discs deftly and fast, and it looks so easy, but it isn't. In fact, I have never succeeded in re-creating it at home – either the small discs are too thick or too thin, they get holed and they don't stick together, or the big disc falls apart and so on. Although it is not quite the same as *warkah*, filo can be substituted.

Filo pastry can be baked, pan-fried and deep-fried. Being very thin, it is very crispy and crackly when cooked. Some recipes require it to be boiled when the texture is soft.

BOREK

Small stuffed pastries

The royal chefs of the Ottomans vied with each other to produce the most memorable creations for their masters. He that achieved such a feat was showered with accolades, praise and on occasions gold and jewels. Adrenalin ran freely in the Ottoman kitchen, and great things transpired. One of them was a series of tiny pastries in myriad shapes and fillings. They were called *boreks* and soon became highly popular in all parts of the seventeenth-century Ottoman world. The pastry was always translucently thin and was based on filo or *warkah*. The names in each country varied slightly, producing a series of permutations on the original *borek*. The shapes were many, and the fillings equally varied. To explain and describe this enormous range, I have tabulated them on pages 68 and 70.

DOUGHS AND PASTRIES

Pastry	Country	Dough
borek/borekler/ boregler	Turkey	Yufka
burekakia	Greece	filo/phyllo/fila
boreg	Armenia	phyllo
boreka	Israel	
burak/sambusak	The Gulf	ajeen
	The Levant	
samboosek	Egypt	gullash
Briek/brik	Tunisia	madsouka
bourek	Algeria	dioul
briouat	Morocco	warka/ouarka
	Iran	qotab/koteh

The Shapes

triangle
square or parcel or pillow
cylinder
cigar or cigarette (cigara)

spiral or coil (burma borek)
scimitar or half-moon
semicircle
sphere or ball

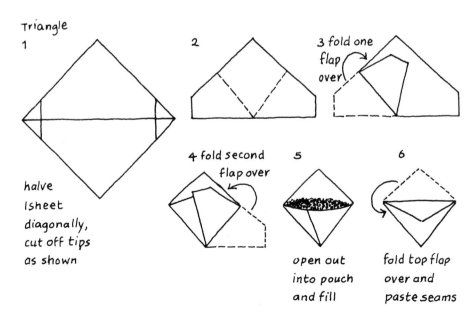

Triangle

1 — halve 1 sheet diagonally, cut off tips as shown

2

3 fold one flap over

4 fold second flap over

5 open out into pouch and fill

6 fold top flap over and paste seams

Square or parcel or pillow

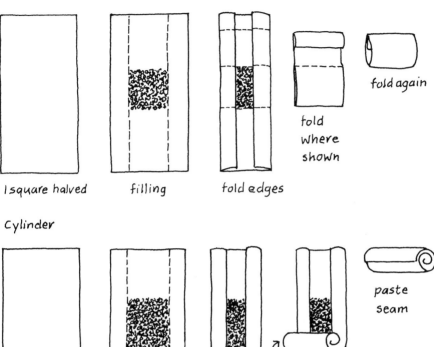

I square halved   filling   fold edges

fold
where
shown

fold again

Cylinder

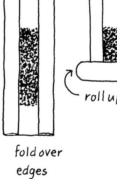

I square halved   put filling   fold over
                    into area shown   edges

roll up

paste
seam

Cigar or cigarette

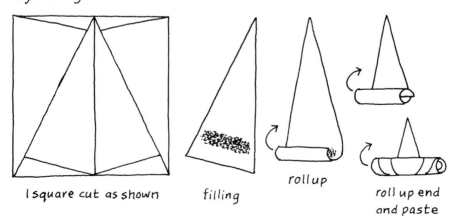

I square cut as shown   filling

roll up

roll up end
and paste

TRADITIONAL COMBINATIONS

Name	Filling	Shape
ispanakli boregi	spinach	triangle
bohca boregi	herbs and cream cheese	sphere
puf boregi	minced meat	shaped or layers
cigara boregi	cheese	cigarette or cigar
burma boregi	any	coil
sanbusak boregi	any	scimitar
su boregi	any	boiled layers

Dimensions

In the world of *boreks*, small is beautiful. Small also requires great skill to maintain this beauty. *Boreks* as small as 1 inch (2·5 cm) are perfect mezzeh or canapé food, and very attractive they look. Equally *boreks* can be as large as 6 inches (15 cm), when each one is virtually a meal in itself. The size of most *boreks* is somewhere in between.

The Fillings

Your imagination is your limitation regarding *borek* fillings. Traditional examples include minced or chopped meat, poultry, fish or seafood, *kibbeh*, cheese, egg and mashed or chopped vegetables such as potato or spinach, rice, lentils and nuts. Suitable recipes in this book for *borek* fillings include the uncooked meat mixture of *koftit ferakh* (page 100) and kibbeyets (page 83) *keksheh bil hout* (page 113) drained and mashed, *nachbous* (page 111), and the filling of *spanokopitta* (page 74), *tyropitta* and *kotopitta* (page 75).

Cooking

Best results are obtained by deep-frying or baking the *boreks*, but pan-frying and, in some cases, boiling are used. Deep fry at 355°F/180°C for 3–5 minutes or until golden; bake at 375°F/190°C/Gas 5 for 5–10 minutes or until golden; pan fry in oil or smen for 5–10 minutes or until golden; boil in plain water for 5–10 minutes.

Spiral

one-third of a square

roll up

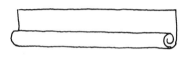

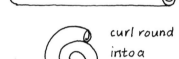

curl round
into a
spiral

Semi-circle and scimitar or half-moon

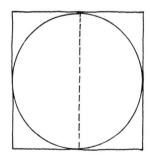 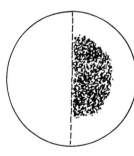 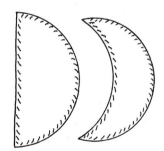

one square or   cut into circle   fold over,   shape
quarter square   and fill   paste   into
                                                 and press   half-moon
                                                 edges

BISTEEYA
•

Pigeon pie

Bisteeya, sometimes spelled *b'steeya*, *bistilla* or *basteela* and pronounced 'pasteeya', loses considerably in its translation into English. It is indeed pigeon pie, but somehow calling it that does not in any way reveal what a delicious dish it is.

Many Moroccans regard it as their national masterpiece. Certainly it appears whenever there is something to celebrate. The real thing is difficult to make, requiring a couple of days, and the thinnest of *warkah* pastry: layers of it are built up and interleaved with alternate fillings of spicy pigeon and a sweet ground almond paste. This intriguing mixture of savoury, sweet and sour was probably introduced to the Maghreb from Persia over 1,000 years ago. Curiously, though, it is not found in the lands in between.

Bisteeya's traditional shape is round or octagonal, and after baking it is garnished with icing sugar and ground cinnamon. I obtained this recipe from the excellent Bhaja Moroccan restaurant at Marrakesh's Hotel La Momunia. I have simplified it by using filo pastry, which is nearly as good.

Serves 4

either 8 oven-ready pigeons,
weighing around 6oz (175g)
each or 4 poussins, each
weighing around 1lb (450g)
or use equal weight of pheasant,
partridge or grouse
4 tablespoons lemon juice
1 recipe chermoula (see page 34)
4 eggs, scrambled
$\frac{1}{2}$ teaspoon aromatic salt
1 tablespoon finely chopped fresh
  mint
1 tablespoon finely chopped fresh
  coriander
smen or clarified butter, melted
1lb 2oz (500g) packet filo pastry
  (ie 24 sheets of
  12 × 20in/50 × 30cm)

ALMOND FILLING
7oz (200g) ground almonds
4 tablespoons granulated brown
  sugar
1 tablespoon powdered cinnamon
2–3 tablespoons orange-blossom
  or rose water

GLAZE
4 tablespoons Grand Marnier
  liqueur

GARNISH
icing sugar
powdered cinnamon or grated
  nutmeg

1 Skin the pigeons or poussins and make small gashes in the flesh. Rub in the lemon juice and set aside for 2 hours.

2 Make the *chermoula* and cool.

3 In a large non-aluminium casserole dish, rub the *chermoula* into the pigeons, cover and keep in the fridge for at least 24 hours.

4 Next day, preheat the oven to 375°F/190°C/Gas 5. Put the casserole dish into the oven and cook for 30 minutes. Inspect during the cooking to ensure it is dry but not dried up (add a little water if necessary).

5 Remove and cool sufficiently to handle. (Keep the oven on.) Then remove the bones and unwanted matter. Chop the meat into small pieces. Mix in the scrambled egg, salt, mint and coriander.

6 Mix the almond filling ingredients together so that they are crumbly and not too wet.

7 Select a round oven dish about 9 inches (23cm) in diameter. Brush it with melted *smen*.

8 Have a clean damp tea towel ready. Open the filo pastry packet and pull out all twenty-four sheets. Cut them together down to 12 inch (30cm) squares with 12 × 8 inches (30 × 20cm) rectangles.

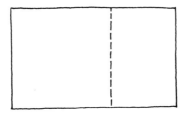

9 Take six of the larger square sheets (covering the rest with a tea towel), brush each with *smen*, and lay them into the oven tray, overlapping as in the diagram. Do not press too hard. Spread with a layer of pigeon filling. Take eight of the off-cut rectangular sheets and place over the filling, overlapping them so that they form four 12 inch (30cm) squares. Spread with a layer of crumbly almond.

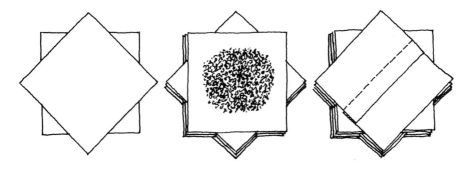

10 Repeat stage 9 until all the sheets and all the fillings are used. Brush the top surface with melted *smen*, then fold the overhanging edges inwards to an octagonal shape. Brush with Grand Marnier.

11 Bake for about 15–20 minutes. It should be pale golden. Remove and carefully ease it out of the oven dish. Invert and replace in the dish, brushing the top with Grand Marnier again. Bake for 10–15 more minutes. Remove when golden brown.

12 Again ease it out of the dish on to a serving plate. Turn it over and brush top once more with Grand Marnier then dust it with icing sugar and a grid of ground cinnamon as shown below for a really traditional look.

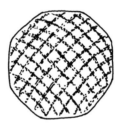

SPANOKOPITTA

Spinach with feta cheese pie

Although I had not intended to include Greek recipes in this book, *spanokopitta* really cannot be omitted. It is a crispy filo pastry pie, traditionally with a filling of spinach, feta cheese and herbs. It is normally made as a large pie which is cut into individual portions, but it can also be made in triangles, discs or coils. This recipe and its two sister recipes below come from Athens' wonderful Hilton Hotel restaurant, the Taverna ta Nissia. Follow the filo instructions for baklava on page 160 (see step 4 opposite).

Serves 4 as a main course, 8 as a starter

1lb 2oz (500g) packet filo pastry
2oz (50g) smen or clarified butter

FILLING
1½lb (675g) spinach, fresh, frozen or canned
2 tablespoons olive or sunflower oil
1 clove garlic, finely chopped

4oz (110g) onion, finely chopped
2 eggs
4 tablespoons each of finely chopped parsley, coriander and mint
½ teaspoon powdered cinnamon
2oz (50g) feta cheese, crumbled
½ teaspoon aromatic salt

1 Make the filling first. Clean and finely chop the fresh spinach. Boil it until cooked (15 minutes), or follow packet or label instructions. Strain.

2 Meanwhile, heat the oil and stir-fry the garlic and onion until golden for about 10 minutes. Add the spinach.

3 Beat the eggs in a bowl, and add the remaining ingredients. Pour into the frying pan and stir-fry just until the egg sets. Remove from the heat and strain.

4 To assemble the pie, follow the baklava method in steps 3, 4 and 5 (see page 161), but, instead of the nuts, spread with the spinach filling. Carry on with stage 6.

5 Cut through the top layers of filo to about halfway through.

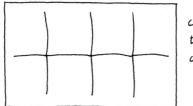

cut through
top layers
as shown

6 To bake, follow stage 8 of the baklava recipe.

7 Cut into individual pieces, and serve hot or cold.

TYROPITTA

Egg and cheese pie

Follow the method for *spanokopitta*, but replace the spinach with 8oz (225g) grated mature cheese.

KOTOPITTA

Minced chicken pie

Follow the method for *spanokopitta*, but replace the spinach with 12oz (350g) minced chicken. Stir-fry this in the oil until cooked as at stage 2.

PASTELLE

Puff pastry pot

These are neat little individual pies that have been cooked by the Jews of the Middle East for centuries. They are now an established Israeli speciality with two traditional fillings, *tatbila* (minced meat) or *khandrajo* (aubergine).

Layered filo pastry can be used, but I prefer thinly rolled puff pastry. The individual pies are about $2\frac{1}{2}$ inches (6cm) in diameter, with a pastry lid which overhangs the pot.

Traditionally the pot is moulded by hand from a small ball, and it will produce a better shape than the modern easy way, using a tart tray.

Makes 12 pastelles

$\frac{1}{2}$ *receipe kiymeh mashwi omani*
  for *tatbila (see page 85)*
  or $\frac{1}{2}$ *recipe muttabel for*
  khandrajo (see page 54)

13oz (370g) packet commercial
  puff pastry
2 eggs, beaten, for glazing

1 Make the filling first, then strain and leave to cool. Meanwhile, pre-heat the oven to 350°F/180°C/Gas 4.

2 Roll out the puff pastry as thinly as you can. To make twelve pies, cut into twenty-four 4 inch (10cm) squares. Press one square into each depression of a twelve-hole tart tin.

3 Fill each square, pressing the filling down.

4 Fit each one with a pastry square lid. Carefully cut round the pie to give it a circular lid which overhangs the pie pot. Remove any spare dough. Ensure each pie is separated from its neighbour. Brush on the beaten egg glaze.

5 Bake for 20 minutes, until the pies are an attractive pale golden colour.

LAHMA BI AJEEN

Arab pizza

A dish which usually surprises first-time visitors to the 'Arab lands' is *lahma bi ajeen*. To all intents and purposes this is a pizza in that it consists of a disc of baked pastry with a spicy meat topping. Everyone assumes this dish is simply a modification of the celebrated Italian pizza. The suprise comes with the discovery that the honours are the other way round. It was not the Italians who invented the pizza, it was the Byzantines. At the height of their empire, over 1,000 years ago, they ruled Greece, southern Italy, Syria and Anatolia (Turkey). This dish was no doubt transported from their capital Constantinople (Istanbul) to all parts of their Empire. It undoubtedly was called pizza, having derived from two Turkish words, *piaz* (onion) and *pitta* (bread).

Normally the *lahma* is a pastry dish of about 6–8 inches (15–20cm) in diameter, upon which can be put a variety of spicy toppings, traditional amongst which is this meat recipe, which I encountered in Abu Dhabi.

Makes 8 lahmas

1 recipe khoubiz bread (see page 153) unbaked

THE TOPPING
$\frac{1}{2}$ *recipe kiymeh mashwi omani (see page 85) NB: The spice mixture can be used, reduced or omitted to taste.*

Prepare the bread as on page 153 but bake for only 4–5 minutes. Turn over and spread with topping. Bake for a further 4–5 minutes. This dish can also be grilled, in which case halve the cooking times.

S'FINAH

Miniature pizzas

A tiny and rather elegant version of *lahma bi ajeen* is found all over the Levant and the Gulf. Make these exactly as the *lahmas* (above) but make the disc size no more than 3 inches (7·5cm) in diameter. I encountered one clever variation of *s'finah* where the disc was given a slightly convex shape, and a quail's egg was broken on top of the filling – it was then baked as normal.

Makes about 20 s'finahs

CHAPTER·6

MEAT DISHES

MAN has been a carnivore since he progressed from eating roots, berries and eggs, to the hunter-gatherer stage more than a million years ago. When he began to farm in the fertile crescent, it was sheep and goats which were bred for fleece and meat as early as 9000 BC. The domestication of cattle did not take place until some 3,000 years later, and ancient Turkey seems to have pioneered this development. Pig has never been an important meat in the Middle East. Small, hairy and black wild pigs undoubtedly existed, but the Jewish *kosher* rules formulated thousands of years ago forbade the consumption of pork. More significantly, Islam followed in the seventh century AD. The animal is considered to be unclean, its flesh the carrier of disease, and a strict orthodox Jew or Moslem would be unable to contemplate the consumption of any part of the pig. The origins of this are obscure. Uncleanliness and disease are not satisfactory reasons, for pork has been the primary meat of the Far East for millennia. The true answer may lie in the fact that pigs, being rooters, simply did not thrive in desert conditions. The few that did, apart from being scarce, may well have been diseased.

All the peoples of the Middle East are voracious meat eaters. The most popular meats are mutton or goat, lamb being a luxury for the special occasion. Beef is permitted and enjoyed, although cows, oxen or buffalo are uncommon. Pork is eaten by the Christian communities and offal is popular with everyone. Jews are not permitted to eat rabbit, or any meat cooked or served with dairy products. The Iranians, on the other hand, have developed a style of cooking in which meat is marinated in yoghurt.

My selection of recipes includes lamb, beef, veal, pork and rabbit cooked in a wide variety of methods which include skewered kebabs, ground and minced meat, a number of stews or casseroles and grilled or fried items. But the dish which everyone associates with the Middle East is whole roast lamb – *khouzi* – and the recipes for this, and for the smaller leg, are a must for all cooks.

THE KEBAB

Kebabs are now a familiar favourite the world over, and they come in a variety of shapes and sizes. Traditionally, they are made from meat marinated in a mixture of oil and spices then cubed to bite-sized pieces, or pounded with a mortar and pestle and shaped on the skewer. These techniques were perfected in ancient Turkey. The marinade not only gives flavour but tenderizes the meat, which, in the arid Middle East, tends to be tough and stringy. In Western countries meat is very juicy and succulent so the marinade process is for taste only. We can also be more adventurous with our choice of meat, too – lamb, beef, veal, pork, duck and chicken can all be used.

Liver, kidneys and heart can also be cooked as kebabs. Seafood and fish are excellent and, with a little ingenuity, the vegetarian need not be left out. Firm vegetables such as potato, carrot, courgette, cauliflower etc. can be marinated in cubes, then cooked or mashed, spiced and shaped, then grilled.

The best flavour is achieved over charcoal but an indoor oven/grill produces results nearly as good.

SHASHLIK KEBAB

Marinated grilled meat on a skewer

Simple to make and visually attractive, *shashlik* is a tasty combination of skewered marinated meat and vegetables, originating from Armenia, but found all over the Middle East. It is a healthy dish, being low in calories, and high in protein and vitamins (especially if you eat the garnish salad).

Serve as a *mezzeh* item or as a starter on a bed of lettuce topped with mustard and cress and parsley, accompanied by lemon or lime wedges and chilli sauce (harissa, see page 51) or yogurt (see page 38). *Shashlik* can also make a fine main course if served with rice (*chelow*, see page 148) and *pitta* bread (see page 154). Traditionally the meat would be goat or mutton, but we could substitute lamb, pork or veal – but best of all is top-quality beef. For a change try king prawns or chicken breast (cook these for less time than for meat).

Serves 4

1lb (450g) topside of beef or 1 inch
  (2·5cm) thick fillet or sirloin
  steak
1 red capsicum pepper
1 green capsicum pepper
1 Spanish or large onion
4 green chillies (optional)
4 cloves garlic, whole and peeled
  (optional)

MARINADE
4 tablespoons olive oil
1 teaspoon ground cummin
½ teaspoon powdered cassia bark
  or cinnamon
6 tablespoons red wine
1 tablespoon lemon juice
2 teaspoons tomato purée
½ teaspoon puréed or finely
  chopped garlic

1 Thoroughly mix together all the marinade ingredients.

2 Discard any gristle, fat etc from the meat and cut into twenty cubes a minimum size of 1 inch (2·5 cm) each. (Use any off-cuts for something else.)

3 Cover the meat with the marinade, then cover with cling film and leave to stand in the fridge for a minimum of 6 hours, a maximum of 24.

4 After the meat has marinated, cut the red pepper to obtain eight diamond or square 1 inch (2·5 cm) shapes. Do the same with the green pepper. Separate the layers of the onion and cut twenty pieces to the same shape. (Use leftover pepper and onion for something else.)

5 Pre-heat oven to 180°C/350°F/Gas 4, and meanwhile thread the items on to each skewer as follows: onion, meat, green pepper, meat, onion, red pepper, meat, onion, green pepper, meat, onion, red pepper, meat, onion. Put a clove of garlic and/or one green chilli on to each skewer (optional). Ensure all items are close together but not squashed.

6 Place the skewers on to a wire rack and the rack on to an oven tray (drip pan). Baste the skewers with the excess marinade.

7 When the oven is at the correct heat, cook for 8–10 minutes for rare meat, 10–15 for medium, and 15 and more for well done. Alternatively cook under the grill at medium heat with the rack at the lowest level for the same times, or cook over the barbecue.

KOFTAH

Mince balls

Koftah is a type of kebab made from ground meat mixed with herbs and spices, which is shaped into balls and baked or fried. In the Maghreb they are called *kaftah*, in Greece *keftethes*, in Armenia *keufte*, and in the Levant and the Gulf it varies in pronunciation between *kuftah* and *koftah*. The *kofta* is a favourite dish in India, undoubtedly taken there by the Arab and Moslem invaders of long ago. In the Middle East *koftahs* are more likely to be served without a sauce, but with a selection of salads, dips and bread.

An Arab variation of this dish is called *lahmah-kafta bil karaz*. The lamb is ground, rolled out to cherry-sized balls, then grilled to a dark colour. These are served in a gravy along with firm sour black local cherries, and the fun is to identify which is cherry and which is meat ball! For a gravy, use the sauce recipe on page 84.

Serves 4 (24 koftas)

$1\frac{1}{2}lb$ (675g) topside of beef or lean
    chump or leg of lamb, weighed
    after stage 1
2–6 cloves garlic, chopped
    (optional)
1–3 teaspoons baharat
2 teaspoons dried mint

1 tablespoon chopped fresh
    fenugreek leaves (Yemeni
    option)
1 tablespoon chopped fresh
    coriander leaves
4 fresh chillies, chopped (Tunisian
    option)
$\frac{1}{2}$ teaspoon aromatic salt

1 Prepare the meat by removing unwanted matter. Cut into smallish pieces suitable for grinding.

2 Mix all the ingredients together then run them through a mincer or food processor to a fine, well-blended, sticky texture. You will achieve the same texture pounding by hand, but it is a chore.

3 Divide the mixture into four, then subdivide into six (to obtain a total of twenty-four). Roll into balls.

4 Place on an oven tray and put into an oven pre-heated to 325°F/160°C/Gas 3 for 15 minutes. Alternatively, grill or barbecue. Serve with rice and relishes such as *dukkah* (see page 52).

KIBBEH (*Ground meat and cracked wheat paste*)

Kibbeh is a mixture of ground meat, cracked wheat (burghul), onion and spices. It originated thousands of years ago in the fertile crescent and to this day it is regarded as the national dish of Lebanon and Syria. Simple in concept, it has many variations, particularly in spicing. The Iraqi versions are called *koubbah*, in Armenia *keuftas*, which use pork. Egyptian variants are made from coarsely ground rice instead of burghul and they are called *hamda*. The ancient Jewish variants are made from *matzo* (ground bread), and are known as *masso*. *Kibbeh* can be eaten raw (an acquired taste) or fried as rissoles. It is also used as a stuffing in vegetables (see page 122). Serve all the *kibbeh* varieties with a salad, plain yoghurt and *khoubiz* bread.

BASIC KIBBEH

Serves 4 as an accompanying dish

4oz (110g) burghul (processed cracked wheat)
8oz (225g) leg of lamb, weighed after stage 2
2oz (50g) onion, roughly chopped

1 Rinse and strain the burghul.

2 Now prepare the lamb. Remove all fat, gristle and undesirable pieces. Cut into chunks.

3 Mix meat, moist burghul and the onion together, then pulse it in the food processor until you obtain a paste-like texture.

4 Scrape it out on to a work surface. You'll find it rather sticky. This is as it should be, but it makes it tricky to complete the shaping stage. The answer is to use a bowl of warm water to keep them smooth.

5 Roll into balls, or sausage or rissole shapes, and deep-fry for 10 minutes.

KIBBEYETS

Minced meat in a kibbeh shell

The most intriguing use of *kibbeh* is to use it as a casing around a different minced meat filling. This Syrian recipe has been handed down from mother to daughter for countless generations. The woman who gave it to me explained that in her grandmother's day the eligibility of potential wives was determined by their ability to produce this dish. Its centre should be soft and succulent whilst its outside should be crackling crisp. Deep-frying produces the best results.

Serves 4

1 recipe kibbeh (opposite)

FILLING
8oz (225g) fillet steak or leg of lamb (traditional) or pork (Armenian) or veal, weighed after stage 1

4 tablespoons smen
2oz (50 g) onion, finely chopped
2oz (50 g) pine nuts
1 teaspoon baharat
1 teaspoon salt

1 To make the filling, remove all fat, gristle and undesirables from the meat of your choice. Cut into chunks to enable it to be minced easily.

2 Run it through a fine mincer.

3 Heat the *smen*, and stir-fry the onion for 5 minutes or so. Add the mince and stir-fry for 10 minutes.

4 Run the pine nuts through the mincer and add them, the *baharat* and salt to the meat. Mix well then place in a strainer and allow to go cold.

5 To make the *kibbeh* shells, proceed to the end of stage 4 of the *kibbeh* recipe. Divide the paste into twelve equal balls (of about ping-pong ball size). Smooth them using the water and keep your hands clean. Have the cold filling to hand.

6 Hold one ball in one hand then poke the index finger of your other hand into the ball and work it gently around until you have made a thin-shelled pouch about the size of a tennis ball. If it breaks, start again, but persevere until you succeed (it gets easier with practice!).

7 Carefully spoon in the filling until the shell is two-thirds full, then press the shell down to close. Carefully shape it to a rounded cylinder or cone. (If the shape is moulded into discus shapes they are called *or'rus*.)

8 Pre-heat deep-frier to 330–340°F (about 170°C, ie not too hot), then put in four *kibbeyets*. Fry until the case is crispy and golden brown (6–8 minutes should be enough).

ZAYTUN MECHOUI

Olive-studded meat balls

This dish is unique to Tunisia and it is decorative and unusual. I am not certain of its origins, neither was the chef who showed me his method of making the dish, but he assured me it was a dish which had been a favourite of the Tunisian sultans and their courts way back in time. The dish is served as a main course and each portion consists of a number of *zaytun mechoui*. They are made by pressing halved olives on to meat balls, dipping them in flour, eggs and breadcrumbs, and deep-frying them. They are served with a spicy tomato-based sauce and are garnished with rings of black and green olives, and fresh oregano. Reflecting an ancient Carthaginian link which Tunis has with Sicily, this dish goes exceedingly well with rigatone (large macaroni) or fettucine (wide flat pasta strips) and a topping of Parmesan cheese and fresh herbs.

Serves 4

MEAT BALLS
1½lb (675 g) sirloin steak, weighed
   after stage 1
2 fried eggs, with soft yolks
4–6 cloves garlic, chopped
6 oz (175 g) onion, finely chopped
1 teaspoon freshly ground black
   pepper
½ teaspoon aromatic salt
1 tablespoon finely chopped fresh
   coriander
72 green olives

plain white flour
2 raw eggs, beaten
dry breadcrumbs

SAUCE
4–6 canned plum tomatoes
1 red capsicum pepper
2–4 cloves garlic
harissa (see page 51), to taste
   (optional)
2 tablespoons olive oil
½ pint (300ml) stock or water

1 It is best to make the sauce before you start the balls, either keeping it warm or letting it cool down (it freezes well), then reheating as required. Purée the tomato, red pepper, garlic and harissa (if wanted). Stir-fry the purée in the hot oil for 5 minutes, then add the stock or water. (When simmering it is ready to serve over the studded meat balls.)

2 Prepare the steak for the meat balls by removing all unwanted fat, gristle etc, then cut into chunks.

3 The eggs are best cold, and they act as very efficient binding agents. Put them, the meat and the garlic into a food processor and pulse into a coarse paste. Alternatively use a hand mincer, putting it through at least twice.

Serves 4

$1\frac{1}{2}$ *lb (675g) stewing steak*
4 tablespoons smen or vegetable oil
8oz (225g) onion, chopped
1 teaspoon ground cummin

4–6 canned tomatoes
1 red capsicum pepper
ground black pepper and salt to
taste

1 Remove all fat, gristle and undesirables from the meat, then cut it into $1\frac{1}{2}$ inch (4cm) cubes.

2 Heat the *smen* or oil, and stir-fry the onion and ground cummin for 5 minutes. Add the meat and stir-fry for 10 minutes to 'seal' it.

3 Transfer these ingredients and the tomatoes and red pepper to a saucepan as described above, adding approximately the same volume of boiling water, and bring it to the boil on the stove. Simmer for 30 minutes, stirring occasionally.

4 Put the couscous (as described on page 142) into a muslin-lined sieve which fits on to the meat saucepan. Put the lid on the sieve and continue to simmer the stew for 20 minutes more. The steam cooks and flavours the couscous. Keep fluffing it up with a fork about every 5 minutes.

5 When the couscous is cooked to your liking, remove it from the muslin liner and carefully pile it up into a cone shape in a serving dish. Put it in a warmer until you are ready to serve.

6 Meanwhile season the stew with pepper and salt, then strain it, putting the liquid into a gravy boat.

7 Make a depression in the couscous and nestle the dry stew inside it.

8 To serve, place the dish on the table allowing the diners to help themselves and add gravy to their liking.

FEZ-STYLE COUSCOUS MEAT STEW

For this spicy variation, follow the recipe above, but using a combination of steak and *merguez* or similar sausage (see page 62) – about 50/50 – totalling $1\frac{1}{2}$ lb (675g) prepared. This should be about two sausages.

Serves 4

1 Prepare the meat as in stage 1, and mix with the sausages, removed from their casings and chopped.

2 Add 2–4 cloves garlic and 1 tablespoon *ras-el-hanout* at stage 2.

3 Proceed with the following stages. Garnish with chopped fresh coriander.

CHOLENT or AD'FINA

Slow-cooked stew

The origins of this dish are a little obscure, but it is certainly exclusive to the Jews and it will be found in every Jewish household all over the world. It is a dish normally eaten on the Sabbath, when no work, including cooking, is permitted. It was probably originated by the medieval Sephardic Jews of Palestine (where the spicy variation, or optional ingredients below, is called *ad'fina* or *gefeenah*). Migrant Jews took it to Europe and later the USA, where over the centuries it became the less spicy *cholent*. Both versions are now very much established as Israeli favourites.

Serves 4

$1\frac{1}{2}$lb (675g) stewing steak, weighed after stage 1
8oz (225g) potatoes
8oz (225g) total-weight carrots and/or parsnip and/or turnip
4 tablespoons vegetable oil
1–4 cloves garlic, finely chopped
8oz (225g) onion, finely chopped

1 inch (2·5cm) cube fresh ginger, chopped (optional)
2–4 teaspoons baharat (optional)
4oz (110g) pearl barley or whole wheat
salt and black pepper to taste
fresh coriander or parsley, coarsely chopped

1 Remove all fat, gristle and undesirables from the meat, then cut it into 2 inch (5cm) cubes.

2 Wash and peel the potatoes, then cut into $1\frac{1}{2}$ inch (4cm) pieces. Keep in a bowl of cold water until required.

3 Wash and peel the carrots and/or parsnips and/or turnips and cut into 1 inch (2·5cm) pieces. Add to the potatoes in their bowl.

4 Heat the oil. Stir-fry the garlic for 1 minute, then add the onion and continue stir-frying for 5 or 6 minutes.

5 Add the meat and stir-fry to 'seal' it for about 10 minutes.

6 Transfer the meat stir-fry to a casserole dish or electric slow cooker, adding the remaining ingredients and mixing well. Add approximately the same volume of boiling water. Put the lid on the casserole and put it into an oven pre-heated to 375°F/190°C/Gas 5. Cook for 30 minutes then inspect and stir. Reduce heat to 250°F/120°C/Gas $\frac{1}{2}$, and leave for 3 or 4 hours. Season with salt and pepper.

7 To serve the traditional way, strain off the gravy and place it in a gravy boat. Put equal quantities of the meat on each of four dining plates and arrange the remaining ingredients around the meat. Garnish with fresh coriander or parsley. This is a meal in itself and needs no side dishes.

KORESH or KORAK

Lamb in a creamy aromatic sauce

This dish originated in ancient Persia. Literally meaning 'sauce poured over rice', it appears at nearly every meal, and in many guises. The *korak* is the thicker version, containing meat, poultry or vegetables, often dried fruit and nuts. Sometimes yoghurt is used and the dish is spiced, but the spicing is subtle and aromatic, never overwhelming and hot. The tastes combine sweet and sour and the textures are soft and crunchy.

Serves 4

1½lb (675g) leg of lamb, weighed after stage 1
4 tablespoons smen or vegetable oil
8oz (225g) onion, chopped
1 teaspoon turmeric
1 teaspoon powdered cinnamon
⅓ teaspoon ground cloves

½ teaspoon freshly ground black pepper
4oz (110g) dried apricots and/or prunes and/or firm, sour, fresh cherries
½–1 teaspoon sumak (optional)
2–4 loumi (dried limes)
aromatic salt to taste

1 Prepare the meat, discarding all fat, gristle and undesirables. Cut into 1¼ inch (4 cm) pieces.

2 Heat the *smen* or oil to just below smoking point. Stir-fry the onions for 5 or 6 minutes, then add the turmeric, cinnamon, cloves and pepper, stir-frying for a further 5 minutes.

3 Transfer the above fried items to a lidded casserole and mix in the meat, the dried fruit if being used (but not any fresh fruit yet), the *sumak* (for an ultra-sour taste) and the *loumi*. Place the casserole in the oven preheated to 375°F/190°C/Gas 5 and cook for 20 minutes.

4 Remove, inspect and stir. Add a little water as required, and return to the oven for 20 more minutes. Remove and stir in any fresh fruit at this stage and return to the oven for a final cooking of 10 minutes minimum, or until it is to the tenderness of your liking. Salt to taste. Serve with rice.

LABAN UMMO or MANSAAF

Lamb cooked with yoghurt

This is another very ancient dish. Bedouin tribespeople regarded water as their most precious asset, and it could not always be spared for cooking. Thus milk was sometimes the cooking medium. Often this meant killing a young animal and using its mother's milk (*ummo* in Arabic). Today the dish uses thickened yoghurt. It is found in Syria and Lebanon, where it is called *laban* (yoghurt) *ummo*. In Jordan and the Gulf, virtually the same dish is called *mansaaf*, whilst in the Palestine area it is *mansi*.

Serves 4

EITHER
1½lb (675g) leg of lamb, cubed, weighed after stage 1 to make laban ummo
OR
2½lb (1·3kg) leg of lamb, whole, trimmed of fat to make mansaaf
PLUS
2–4 cloves garlic, chopped
12oz (350g) onion, chopped

1 teaspoon ground allspice
1 teaspoon baharat (for mansaaf only)
4 tablespoons smen or vegetable oil
½ pint (300ml) clear stock or water
10oz (300g) laban (yoghurt)
1 tablespoon cornflour
milk
salt to taste
1 tablespoon chopped fresh mint and/or fresh coriander

1 Trim the lamb of all unnecessaries. Cut to 1½ inch (4cm) cubes for *laban ummo*. For *mansaaf*, merely trim off as much fat as possible, keeping the leg whole.

2 Place the meat, garlic, onion, allspice, *baharat* and *smen* with the water or clear stock in a large lidded casserole and put into the oven pre-heated to 375°F/190°C/Gas 5. Cook for 20 minutes, inspect, stir (the *laban ummo*), and cook for a further 20 minutes.

3 Whilst the lamb is in the oven mix the yoghurt with the cornflour in a saucepan. Beat well then heat up on the stove, stirring continuously until it will thicken no more. Add milk little by little if it thickens too much.

4 Mix this into or put over the lamb at the end of stage 2 and add salt to taste. Return to the oven for at least 10 more minutes. Serve when the meat is as tender as you want it. Garnish with fresh mint and/or coriander. Serve with a rice dish.

MISHMISHEYA

Veal with apricots

This dish is clearly of Persian origin and compares interestingly with the *koresh* recipe on page 89, although it is, in fact, an Algerian recipe. *Mishmish* means 'apricot' in Arabic, but all kinds of dried or fresh fruit can be used. Here fresh apricots are made into a paste and the meat is veal, but it works very well with pork too.

Serves 4

1½lb (675g) leg of veal or pork, weighed after stage 1
4 tablespoons smen or vegetable oil
2 cloves garlic, finely chopped
1 inch (2·5cm) cube fresh ginger, finely chopped
8oz (225g) onion, finely chopped
1 teaspoon ground allspice

1 teaspoon powdered cinnamon
1 teaspoon ground coriander
1 teaspoon ground cummin
a little stock or water
10oz (300g) fresh apricots or peaches
salt to taste
1 tablespoon brown sugar (optional)

1 Prepare the meat, discarding all fat, gristle and undesirables. Cut it into 1 inch (2·5cm) cubes.

2 Heat the oil and stir-fry the garlic for 1 minute. Add the ginger and stir-fry for a further minute. Add the onion and continue stir-frying for 5 minutes or so.

3 During stage 2, mix the allspice, cinnamon, coriander and cummin with enough water to make a runny paste, then add to the frying pan. Mix well.

4 Pre-heat oven to 375°F/190°C/Gas 5. Put the meat and fried ingredients into a lidded casserole with a little stock or water. Cook for 20 minutes. Remove, inspect and stir. Add more stock or water if required. Return to oven and cook for a further 20 minutes.

5 During stage 4, peel, halve and stone the apricots or peaches. If they are very soft, mash with a fork. If firm, use the blender or food processor.

6 Remove the casserole from the oven, and stir the puréed fruit in, salt to taste and add the sugar (optional). Return to the oven for a further 10 minutes. Serve with couscous.

KIRSHUH

Heart, kidney and liver stir-fry

Being great meat-eaters, all the Arab countries have tasty ways of using offal. This Yemeni stir-fry is very curry-like, which is typical, because of the Yemeni's ancient trading links with India, and its large migrant Indian population. There are no strict rules as to which offal and which spices should be used, so follow this recipe as a guide and adjust ingredients to suit your palate.

Serves 4

$1\frac{1}{2}$*lb (675 g) heart, kidney or liver, or combination, from lamb, calf, beef, pig (but not in the Yemen!) or poultry, weighed after stage 2*
4 tablespoons vegetable oil
6–10 cloves garlic, finely chopped
2 inch (5cm) cube ginger, finely chopped
8oz (225g) onion, finely chopped
4–6 canned plum tomatoes, chopped
salt and black pepper to taste
1 tablespoon chopped fresh coriander

SPICES
1 teaspoon turmeric
2 teaspoons ground coriander
1 teaspoon ground cummin
1 teaspoon baharat

1 Mix the spices together with enough water to make a paste and set aside.

2 Prepare the offal, discarding fat and tubes etc. Cut into bite-sized cubes.

3 Heat the oil and stir-fry the garlic for 1 minute, then add the ginger and stir-fry for a further minute. Add the spice paste and stir-fry for 2 more minutes. Add the onion, stir-fry for 5 minutes or so, then add the offal.

4 Stir-fry for 10 more minutes, adding a little water to prevent sticking.

5 Then add the tomatoes, salt and pepper to taste, and fresh coriander. Serve after 10–15 minutes' simmering.

ARNHAB CHERMOULA

Spicy marinated spit-roast rabbit

Chermoula or *tchermita* is a paste made from red and gold spices bound with olive oil, onion and garlic. It is used as a marinade base for fish, poultry, meat or game which is subsequently grilled. A visitor to the ancient Moroccan markets – the *medinas* – is bound to be drawn to the open-air braziers of the street food traders who take some meat pieces from a marinade, deftly skewer them and grill them while you wait.

The ingredients will vary from trader to trader and day to day. I have had fish, chicken, pigeon, rabbit, mutton and goat – and more. After one rather chewy, highly spiced occasion, I found I had just eaten camel!

Serves 4

a 3–3½lb (1·3–1·5kg) whole rabbit, skinned, gutted, ready to cook
4–6 tablespoons vinegar, any type

1 recipe chermoula marinade (see page 34)
watercress, parsley and other herbs to garnish

1 Keep the rabbit in one piece, then wash it inside and out, dry and remove unwanted fat, membrane, etc. Make small slashes in the deep flesh with the tip of a sharp knife.

2 Rub in the vinegar and leave the rabbit for an hour or two. The vinegar 'de-greases' the meat and allows the marinade to soak in better.

3 Take the pre-made marinade and rub it thoroughly into the meat, then cover and put in the fridge for up to 24 hours (a minimum of 6).

4 The best way to cook this is on a spit over charcoal. Depending on the variables it will be perfectly cooked after 15 minutes and before 25, but inspection will tell. Alternatively use your oven and if it has a spit rotisserie, so much the better. If not, use a wire rack on an oven tray. Pre-heat oven to 350°F/180°C/Gas 4.

5 Shake off excess marinade, keeping it aside, then put the whole rabbit on to the skewer or oven rack (oven tray beneath to catch the drips), then put it into the oven. Roast for between 20 and 30 minutes, basting with excess marinade in the early stages. Inspect and test at the later stages, removing from the heat when it is to your liking.

6 Either serve whole on a central serving dish, or cut it into portions. Garnish and serve with rice or couscous, and spicy dips such as *harissa* and *dukkah* (see pages 51 and 52).

KHOUZI or M'CHOUI

Whole roasted lamb

No cookbook on Middle Eastern cookery would be complete without a recipe for roasted whole lamb, the traditional Arab ceremonial dish. When I was quite young, a middle-aged friend used to thrill me with tales of feasts held especially for him when in Arabia negotiating with villagers over oil rights. Invariably it would be roast lamb, and as guest of honour he would be expected to eat two great delicacies – the eyes and the testicles. He never got over his squeamishness, but eat them he did, and with apparent gusto, for he could have caused enormous offence. (You are not obliged to cook the 'delicacies'!)

In Morocco the dish is called *m'choui* (from the Arabic word to grill). The carcass is marinated inside and out with spicy *chermoula* paste. It is given as an option here.

For *fakhid kharouf*, an everyday version, use a $3\frac{1}{2}$–4 lb (1·5–1·8 kg) leg of lamb on the bone, and cook it at the same temperature for $1\frac{1}{2}$–2 hours.

To calculate the cooking time of a whole carcass, use the formula for a leg joint, eg $\frac{1}{2}$ hour per 1lb (450g). Remember it has four leg joints so divide the total carcass weight by four, then multiply by $\frac{1}{2}$ hour. An 8lb carcass will therefore take 1 hour to cook, and a 12lb carcass $1\frac{1}{2}$ hours. These are minimum cooking times and the lamb will be pink.

Serves 16–20

1 baby lamb of 8–12lb (3·6–5·4kg), oven-ready
2 tablespoons za'atar
2 tablespoons chopped fresh coriander or parsley

COATING SAUCE FOR KHOUZI
$\frac{1}{2}$pt (300ml) olive or vegetable oil
4 tablespoons baharat

COATING SAUCE FOR M'CHOUI
$\frac{1}{2}$pt (300ml) olive or vegetable oil
1 recipe chermoula (see page 34)

1 Mix the oil and spices together for either coating, then rub into the oven-ready lamb. Keep any spare aside.

2 Place the lamb on to an oven rack and into the oven preheated to 325°F/160°C/Gas 3. Put an oven tray underneath to catch drips.

3 Calculate your cooking time, $\frac{1}{2}$ hour per 1lb (450g), so roughly 1–$1\frac{1}{2}$ hours. Turn and baste with spare coating sauce every 20–30 minutes.

4 Because of the variations in oven temperatures you must check on the tenderness of your meat by inspecting and pricking with the tip of a sharp knife. When it is cooked to your liking, let it rest for 20–30 minutes in a warm oven.

5 Place the whole lamb on a bed of rice, sprinkling on the *za'atar* and fresh coriander or parsley and serve.

CHAPTER·7

POULTRY DISHES

BY 8000 BC, the earliest settlers of the fertile crescent had domesticated the wild chicken, a descendant of the Indian jungle fowl, breeding it for eggs and meat. Since then chicken has always been popular. Today it is roasted with or without stuffing and it is casseroled and stewed. Less conventional cooking methods include frying balls of minced chicken or puréeing it with wheat. But the most remarkable chicken dish in the Middle Eastern repertoire is *pilich dolmasi* from Turkey: minced meat is enclosed within a whole chicken skin and baked. It was devised for the Ottoman rulers. Another dish from royal days is *faisanjan*, a festive dish served at the Persian court, featuring peacock, duck nowadays. Duck does not figure largely in traditional Middle Eastern cookery, although the ancient Egyptians bred them for the tables of the rich. Today duck is more readily available, although as in the West it is relatively expensive.

Small birds of all kinds are devoured with enthusiasm by all Middle Easterners. Sparrows, finches, linnets and larks are caught and grilled as they have been for thousands of years. So too are pheasant, partridge, grouse, quail, dove and pigeon.

Goose has been an Egyptian speciality since Pharaonic times, and modern Israel breeds it prolifically for export. A rather scrawny smallish turkey is found in Turkey although, in fact, turkey did not originate there. The Turks themselves call it *hindi* (or Indian), probably because turkeys originated in America, at first *thought* to be India. How we came to call it 'turkey' is speculation. Perhaps an English ambassador on a visit to the Ottoman court was feasted on turkey. He may have been shown the strutting fowl with its curious gobble-gobble conversation and its pompous, puffed-up appearance. In his explanation to the English court, the ambassador may have likened the bird to the sultan himself – and the name stuck.

DJEJ MECHOUI

Roast chicken

Roast chicken is as popular in the Middle East as it is in the West. There are many variations, ranging from unstuffed and unspiced, much as we would eat them, to heavily spiced and stuffed with *couscous* – for example, *djej m'ahmar*, Algerian style, or *dajaj m'ashi*, Arab style.

In this recipe I have started with basic roast chicken, minimally spiced, and (optionally) more heavily spiced in a recipe from the Yemen. In the Middle East the cooking would be over charcoal, here I use an oven.

Serves 4

1 oven ready roasting chicken,
about 3½lb (1·5kg)

MILD MARINADE
6fl oz (175ml) olive oil
4 tablespoons fresh lemon juice
2 teaspoons aromatic salt
1 teaspoon freshly milled black
pepper

SPICY MARINADE (ALL GROUND)
½ teaspoon turmeric
1 teaspoon cummin
1 teaspoon coriander
1 teaspoon baharat
2 teaspoons dried mint

1 Check that the cavity is empty. Place the chicken on an oven tray.

2 Mix the marinade then rub all over the chicken. Leave it for 2 hours minimum and 24 maximum. Baste from time to time if possible.

3 Preheat the oven to 375°F/190°C/Gas 5. Put the chicken on to an oven rack over the oven tray, basting with the marinade. Pour off excess marinade for later use.

4 Roast for 20 minutes per lb (450g). Baste every 15 minutes with the spare marinade.

5 On the hour for a 3½lb (1·5kg) bird, increase the heat to 425°F/220°C/ Gas 7, and give it a final 10 minutes at that heat.

6 Remove the chicken from the oven, and let it rest for 15 minutes in a warmer.

RIGHT, CLOCKWISE FROM THE TOP: *Kibbeyets* (minced meat in a kibbeh shell) page 83, *Barbari* (Iranian bread) page 155, *Mishmisheya* (veal with apricots) page 91, *Lahma-Kafta Bil Karaz* (miniature meat balls) page 81, *Tahdig* (rice crust) page 149, *Arnhab Chermoula* (roast rabbit) page 93, *Riz El Tammar* (rice with dates) page 151.

DJEJ M'AHMAR

Couscous-stuffed roast chicken with red sauce

This is a favourite dish from North Africa. In this Algerian version, the chicken is glazed with honey and the *couscous* contains sultanas. The outcome is a delicious savoury-sweet combination. It is served with a lovely red sauce, the *m'ahmar*.

Serves 4

Chicken and marinade of choice
  as for djej mechoui (opposite)
4 tablespoons clear honey

STUFFING
6oz (175g) pre-cooked couscous
2oz (50g) pine nuts
2oz (50g) sultanas
2oz (50g) whole almonds
20 strands saffron
2 tablespoons warm milk

SAUCE
4 tablespoons smen
2 teaspoons paprika
1 teaspoon cummin seeds
$\frac{1}{2}$ *pint (300ml) chicken stock or*
  water
2 tablespoons tomato purée
salt

1 Mix all the stuffing ingredients together, then stuff the chicken.

2 Follow the *djej mechoui* recipe to the end of stage 4.

3 Meanwhile make the sauce. Heat the *smen* and stir-fry the paprika and cummin seeds for 1 minute. Add the chicken stock or water and the tomato purée. Salt to taste. Bring to the boil and then simmer for 30 minutes or so until it is reduced by one-third. Add the saffron strands to the warm milk and leave for 10 minutes or until the milk has turned a golden yellow, then add to sauce.

4 At the end of stage 4, glaze the chicken with the honey and follow stages 5 and 6.

5 Pour the hot sauce over the chicken, or serve it in a gravy boat.

LEFT, CLOCKWISE FROM THE TOP: *Siman Bil Kibbeh* (stuffed quail) page 104, *Tagine Djej Bil Tamar Wa Assal* (chicken with dates and honey) page 101, *Djej M'ahmar* (stuffed roast chicken with red sauce in the accompanying jug) above, *Cerkez Tavagu* (Circassian chicken) page 103, Plain Couscous, page 142.

DAJAJ M'ASHI

Roast chicken stuffed with rice

This particular recipe is from the Saudi Arabia capital city of Riyadh.

Serves 4

Chicken and marinade of choice
 as for djej mechoui (see page
 96)

STUFFING
6oz (175g) cooked basmati rice
2oz (50g) onion, chopped and fried

2–4 cloves garlic, chopped and
 fried
1 teaspoon powdered cinnamon
2oz (50g) chopped almonds

1 Mix all the stuffing ingredients together, then stuff the chicken.

2 Follow the *djej mechoui* recipe thereafter.

PILICH DOLMASI

Stuffed filleted minced chicken

This is a dish devised in sixteenth-century Turkey to gratify the opulent Ottoman sultans. It invites comment, and is therefore ideal for dinner parties. The chicken appears to be a normal 'roast chicken' and, without giving the game away, carving should take place with some ceremony in front of the guests. The talking point is the fact that this chicken has no bones. Not only that, the meat is minced and combined with a mixture of nuts, herbs and spices, so it carves into neat slices.

The difficulty lies in removing the chicken skin in one piece. You can do it yourself, but it is tricky and can tear or hole easily. A good butcher will oblige. If there are a few small holes in the skin, smooth them down on to the ground meat.

Serves 4

skin from a 1½–2lb (675g–900g)
  poussin

STUFFING
the flesh, liver, kidney and heart
  of the poussin
8oz (225g) chicken breast
8oz (225g) leg of veal
2oz (50g) pine nuts
2–4 cloves garlic, chopped
2oz (50g) onion, chopped

1 teaspoon powdered cinnamon
1 teaspoon ground allspice
½ teaspoon aromatic salt
½ teaspoon ground black pepper

TO BASTE
4fl oz (100ml) olive oil
2 tablespoons lemon juice
1 teaspoon aromatic salt
1 teaspoon paprika

1 Skin the poussin or get the butcher to do it.

2 Cut the flesh off the bone, and remove all unwanted matter. Cut the meat and the offal ready to mince. (The latter is optional, but adds greatly to the flavour of the dish.)

3 Prepare the chicken breast (discarding the skin) and the veal as in stage 2 above.

4 Put all the meats twice through a fine mincer along with the other stuffing ingredients. Or pulse to a coarse texture in a food processor. Mix well by hand.

5 Take the poussin skin and carefully put the stuffing into it. Don't overfill the skin – leave enough room to fold the openings over and to shape it back to that of a bird. There should be a little stuffing left over which can be frozen.

6 Pre-heat the oven to 375°F/190°C/Gas 5. Put the 'chicken' on an oven tray and baste with one-third of the basting mixture. Cook for 15 minutes.

7 Remove from the oven, and turn the chicken upside down. Baste with one-third more of the basting mixture, and cook for 15 more minutes.

8 Repeat, turning the chicken back the right way up, and using the remaining basting mixture. Cook for a final 15–20 minutes.

9 Remove the chicken from the oven and let it rest for about 10 minutes in a warmer.

10 Put it on a large flat platter so that you can show off while you carve. Serve with a rice dish and vegetables.

KOFTIT FERAKH

•

Fried minced chicken balls

Like their meat counterparts, these minced chicken balls are popular all over the Middle East. This version is from Syria, where they grind pine nuts, cummin seeds and fresh herbs with the meat. In the Gulf they add chilli and turmeric. In Iran they use pistachio nuts instead of pine nuts to make *kufta morgi*, whilst in Turkey the dish is called *tavak koftesi*, and nuts are replaced by breadcrumbs. They can literally vary from cherry size to snooker ball size. To obtain exactly equal sizes divide the mixture into four, then into four again for large-size balls, and into four yet again for cherry-size balls.

Serves 4

*1½lb (675g) chicken breast,
   weighed after stage 1*
2–4 cloves garlic (optional)
2oz (50g) onion, chopped

1 teaspoon ground cummin
2–4 fresh green chillies (optional)
*1 tablespoon chopped fresh
   coriander*

1 Prepare the chicken. Skin it, remove all unwanted matter, and cut into workable pieces.

2 Grind the chicken, garlic, onion, cummin, chillies and coriander together by hand in a fine mincer (twice), or pulse in a food processor until you have a well-blended, glutinous mixture.

3 Heat oven or deep-fryer to 375°F/190°C/Gas 5. Divide the mixture as described above, and cook in oven or fryer for no more than 10 minutes (about 7–8 minutes for cherry size).

4 Drain well and serve with salad, dips, bread etc.

TAGINE DJEJ BIL TAMAR WA ASSAL

Chicken with dates and honey

The *tagine* is the ubiquitous Berber slow-cooked stew. *Tagine* is also the name of the utensil in which the stew is cooked, over charcoal. It is in two parts: the base is a wide, round, earthenware dish, and on top of this sits a tight-fitting conical lid.

The stew itself can include any ingredients of the cook's choice and whatever the contents, the cooking is simple. Add plenty of water and simmer on low heat until it is juicy, tender and the liquid is reduced.

This particular recipe is a northern Moroccan combination of chicken, spices, nuts, honey and dates, its sweet, sour and savoury taste and soft yet crunchy texture reflecting a Persian influence.

Serves 4

$1\frac{1}{2}lb$ (675g) chicken flesh, weighed
   after stage 1
4 tablespoons smen or vegetable
   oil
8oz (225g) onion, chopped
1 clove garlic, freshly chopped
2 teaspoons la kama spice mix

1 teaspoon cummin seeds
2 or 3 bay leaves
12–16 fresh dates, seeded and
   halved
4 tablespoons whole almonds
2 tablespoons honey
aromatic salt to taste

1 Prepare the chicken. Remove the skin and unwanted matter, then cut into bite-sized cubes.

2 In a heavy saucepan heat the *smen* or oil. Fry the onion, garlic, *la kama* and cummin seeds for 15 minutes.

3 Add 1 pint (600ml) boiling water and the bay leaves, and simmer without a lid for about half an hour, during which time the liquid will reduce by about one-third.

4 Then add the chicken meat and continue to simmer for 20 minutes, stirring from time to time. Add a little water if it starts to get too dry.

5 At this stage add the dates, nuts, honey and salt to taste. Simmer for up to 10 more minutes and serve with *couscous* or rice.

SIMSIM DAJ

Sesame-coated chicken pieces

This recipe possibly originated in Jerusalem centuries ago. It has evolved today into a popular Israeli snack or main-course dish, and the modern oven makes it simple to cook. The secret of success lies in roasting the sesame seeds, in removing the chicken skin, and marinating the chicken for a long time.

Serves 4

4 chicken breasts, each around 6oz (175g), weighed after stage 2
2oz (50g) sesame seeds

MARINADE
8 tablespoons sunflower oil

4 tablespoons tahine paste
1 teaspoon paprika
2 cloves garlic, puréed, or 2 teaspoons garlic powder
1 teaspoon aromatic salt

1 Skin and bone the chicken breasts, and cut each into four strips.

2 Mix the marinade ingredients together to achieve a smooth paste, the consistency of ketchup.

3 Put the chicken and marinade into a glass or ceramic bowl, mix well, cover and put aside in the fridge for between 6 and 24 hours.

4 Prior to cooking, pre-heat the oven to 325°F/160°C/Gas 3. Spread the sesame seeds on an oven tray and put into the oven for 10 minutes. Remove and cool (keep the oven on). Spread some seeds on the oven tray.

5 Ensure the chicken pieces are well coated with marinade, then place them one by one into the sesame seed-covered oven tray. Pour excess marinade over the chicken then sprinkle the remaining sesame seeds over the top.

6 Bake in the oven for 20 minutes. Serve with potatoes and vegetables or salad, bread and dips. Lemon wedges and chopped parsley go well.

CERKEZ TAVAGU

Circassian chicken

Strips of cooked chicken breast are encased in a thick, pink, walnut-based purée. The dish originates in the most northern of our Middle Eastern countries, Georgia, but is also found in Armenia and Turkey. It reflects the Caucasian love of walnuts and olive oil, and purée or dip textures. It is rich and attractive and works very well indeed served cold as a *mezzeh* dish, as a starter, as a main-course salad dish, or as a hot main-course dish.

Serves 4

1½lb (675g) chicken breast,
  weighed after stage 1
4 tablespoons olive oil or
  sunflower oil, for frying
5oz (150g) walnuts, shelled
2 slices white or brown bread,
  crusts removed
1 pint (600ml) chicken stock
2oz (50g) carrot, chopped
2–4 cloves garlic, chopped
4oz (110g) onion, chopped

1 red capsicum pepper, seeded
3oz (75g) cream cheese
2 teaspoons paprika
2 tablespoons walnut or hazelnut
  oil
salt and black pepper to taste

GARNISH
chopped parsley
black olives
strips of red capsicum pepper

1 Prepare the chicken breasts by removing all unwanted matter. Cut into strips averaging $2 \times \frac{1}{2}$ inch (5×1cm).

2 Heat the oil in a wok or large frying pan. Stir-fry the chicken strips for about 10 minutes, ensuring that they are evenly and thoroughly cooked. Put aside.

3 Grind the walnuts and bread to a fine crumbly mixture. A food processor gives best results, but pulse in short bursts to minimize the chance of overheating and oiling up the nuts.

4 Boil the chicken stock with the carrot, garlic, onion and red pepper. Simmer for 10 minutes until the vegetables are soft. Strain (reserving the stock) and purée.

5 Combine the walnut–breadcrumb mixture with the vegetable purée and enough stock for a thick creamy texture. Add the cream cheese, paprika, walnut or hazelnut oil and salt and pepper to taste.

6 If you want to serve the dish cold, allow the purée to cool, then mix half of it with all the chicken, putting it into an oval serving dish. Spread

the remaining paste over the top and garnish. Serve with a green salad and *pitta* bread.

7 If you want it hot, slowly heat up the purée (in the wok or large frying pan), stirring to prevent sticking. Add the chicken (and some stock as required), garnish and serve hot with rice and vegetables.

SIMAN BIL KIBBEH

Quail stuffed with ground meat and burghul

The Egyptians are especially fond of stuffed baked or boiled small birds. This recipe for quail stuffed with *kibbeh* is typically Egyptian, and comes from Egypt's best restaurant, the El Nile Rôtisserie in the Nile Hilton Hotel, Cairo.

Serves 4

8 oven-ready quails, around 6oz (175g) each	*1 teaspoon bahar*
1 recipe kibbeh (see page 82)	*6 tablespoons olive oil*
1 teaspoon roasted cummin seeds	*1 tablespoon lemon juice*
	1 teaspoon aromatic salt

1 Pre-heat oven to 325°F/160°C/Gas 3, and check that the cavities of the quail are clean.

2 Mix the *kibbeh* with the cummin seeds and *bahar*, then spoon into the quails. Pull the end flap over the opening.

3 Put the quails into an oven tray. Mix the oil, lemon juice and salt, and use to baste the quail.

4 Put into the oven and bake for about 10 minutes. Then, using basting mixture in the pan, baste and cook for a further 10 minutes.

5 Serve two per person with rice and vegetables.

KESTANEZI HINDI GUVECH

Casseroled turkey with chestnuts

This dish, with its chestnut accompaniment, is quite delicious. Serve with rice and/or vegetables.

Serves 4

1½lb (675g) turkey breast and/or
   thigh, weighed after stage 1
4 tablespoons vegetable oil
8oz (225g) onions, chopped
2 cloves garlic, chopped
4–6 canned plum tomatoes,
   chopped
1 red capsicum pepper, finely
   chopped

1 teaspoon paprika
1 teaspoon powdered cinnamon
½ pint (300ml) water or stock
1lb 2oz (500g) chestnuts, weighed
   after peeling
aromatic salt
ground black pepper

1 Preheat the oven to 375°F/190°C/Gas 5. Prepare the turkey pieces by skinning, boning and cubing the meat into bite-sized pieces.

2 Heat the oil. Stir-fry the onion and garlic for around 10 minutes.

3 Transfer the stir-fry, the turkey meat and the tomatoes, red pepper, paprika and cinnamon to a lidded casserole. Add the water or stock and put into the preheated oven. Cook for 20 minutes.

4 Meanwhile, prepare the chestnuts. If fresh pierce the skins, lightly grill them then peel. If canned use the liquid as well. If you can get them (and they are available in this form all year) use vacuum-packed peeled and cooked chestnuts.

5 Remove the casserole from the oven. Inspect, add more water or stock if it needs it, and stir in the chestnuts. Return to the oven for a further 20 minutes.

6 Remove it again and add salt and pepper to taste. Test the turkey. It should be tender enough to serve.

FAISINJAN KORESH

Duck in a sweet and sour sauce

At the time of the Shahs of Persia, peacock would have been the subject of this dish. At court the whole cooked peacock would be presented on a sea of bright red pomegranate seeds surrounded by saffron yellow rice on a huge jewel-encrusted gold serving dish, adorned with a swaying forest of peacock feathers. A procession of servants would parade dozens of these colourful identical dishes before the assembled all-male court to the accompanying cacophony of reed instruments and drums. At a given sign the marching and trumpeting would cease, the dishes would be held on high, and the Shah would bless them. Then they would be set down amongst the courtiers, who would devour their *faisinjan* with relish. The Shah would sit on his throne observing but not partaking – his own *faisinjan* would come later, out of sight of the court, tested for poison, and in the private company of his *harem*.

Today *faisinjan* is still served at special occasions such as weddings and other times of celebration, and when a special guest visits the household. The main ingredient is wild game such as pheasant or wild duck. The sourness of the pomegranate contrasts with game extremely well. I have modified this dish a little by using domestic duckling which I then roast rather than casserole. This allows you to get rid of the vast amount of fat. The thick gravy is added at the end and if you can't get fresh pomegranate, or if you don't like it, substitute unsweetened redcurrants.

Serves 4

1 *whole duckling or small duck, oven ready, weighing around* $3\frac{1}{2}$–4lb *(1·5–1·8kg)*
4 *tablespoons duck fat*
2 *cloves garlic, finely chopped*
8oz *(225g) onion, chopped*
1 *teaspoon ground cummin*
1 *teaspoon turmeric*
1 *teaspoon powdered cinnamon*
4oz *(110g) ground almonds*
2–4 *tablespoons pomegranate seeds, dry*

1–3 *tablespoons brown sugar*
lemon juice to taste

GARNISH
4oz *(110g) fresh pomegranate seeds, or unsweetened redcurrants*
2 *tablespoons chopped pistachio nuts*
2 *tablespoons chopped fresh coriander*

This recipe is cooked in two operations – roasting the duckling, which takes 30 minutes per lb (450g), or a total of 2 hours for a 4lb (1·8kg) duckling, and cooking the sweet and sour gravy, which takes about 30 minutes.

1 Preheat the oven to 425°F/220°C/Gas 7. Check the cavity is empty, then put the duckling on an oven tray and into the oven for 20 minutes. Then reduce oven temperature to 350°F/180°C/Gas 4.

2 Remove duckling, baste and pour off excess fat. Return to oven for a further 20 minutes.

3 Repeat this three more times over the next hour.

4 During stage 3, make the sauce. Heat the duck fat in a frying pan and stir-fry the garlic and onion for 5 minutes. Add the cummin, turmeric and cinnamon and stir-fry for a further 2 or 3 minutes. Now cool and purée this mixture, adding enough water to get a creamy texture. Return it to the frying pan, and add the ground almonds and enough water to make it into a thick gravy.

5 The distinctive taste in this dish is the sweet and sour achieved traditionally by using pomegranate (sour) and molasses (sweet). In a separate small pan boil $\frac{1}{2}$ pint (300ml) water and put the pomegranate seeds into it. Simmer for 5 minutes, cool then strain, pushing the flesh through the strainer. Return the liquid to the pan. Add the brown sugar, and lemon juice if you want a tarter taste. Add this to the gravy.

6 You should now have about $\frac{3}{4}$ pint (450ml) of thickish gravy.

7 Remove duckling from oven at the end of stage 3 and drain off all fat. Now use about one-third of the gravy to baste the duckling. Return it to the oven for a final 20–30 minutes' cooking (or until tender), during which you should baste it twice more, using all the gravy.

8 To serve, use an attractive oval platter. Centre the duckling and pour all excess gravy over it. Garnish with fresh pomegranate seeds (or redcurrants), pistachio nuts and fresh coriander. Serve with a rice dish.

CHAPTER 8

FISH AND SEAFOOD DISHES

THE Middle East encompasses a vast amount of coastline which encloses many seas including the Mediterranean, Black, Red, Caspian and Arabian seas, and the Persian Gulf. Three great rivers, the Nile, the Tigris and the Euphrates, have dominated the development of civilized man, and there are a number of natural lakes and man-made dams throughout the whole area. Fishing was a well-established routine for the ancient hunter-gatherer tribes, long before man learned about agriculture. Fish were being farmed in pens in natural lakes by the ancient Egyptians, and many examples of fish preserved by smoking and drying have been discovered in the Pyramids.

The warm waters of the Middle East contain thousands of species of fish, of which about 150 are regularly consumed, and hundreds of species of crustaceans and molluscs. Many of these are now available frozen or even (preferably) fresh at good fishmongers. My selection of recipes features a large variety of fish including swordfish, mullet, mackerel, sardines, anchovy, cod, haddock, trout, salmon, sea trout and monkfish, and of seafood including shrimps, king prawns and lobster or crawfish. You can widen this selection yourself by using the fish or seafood of your preference. The cooking methods in this chapter are equally varied and include grilling, barbecuing, casseroling, baking, currying, stewing, frying, mincing and stuffing.

Fish is now recognized as being one of the healthiest foods we can eat. It is high in protein and low in fat.

KILICH SHISH

Skewered swordfish

Walk past any seaside café in Turkey and you will be tantalized by the aroma of fish sizzling over charcoal. Big, fat, skewered cubes of fish drip their oily herbal marinade on to the coals and in a few minutes they are served inside pitta bread for a snack, or with rice and a garlic and lemon dip for a more substantial meal.

Use a large fish with firm white flesh. Swordfish is traditional (and available frozen and fresh in Britain). Alternatives include shark, barracuda or halibut.

Serves 4

2lb (900g) swordfish

MARINADE
6 tablespoons olive oil
2 tablespoons lemon juice
2 oz (50 g) onion, very finely chopped
2 teaspoons paprika
1 teaspoon ground white pepper
½ teaspoon ground bay leaf
½ teaspoon aromatic salt

DIP
6 tablespoons hazlenut oil
2 tablespoons lemon juice
2 tablespoons finely chopped fresh coriander
2–6 cloves garlic, very finely chopped
1 teaspoon coarsely ground black pepper
½ teaspoon aromatic salt

1 Prepare the fish. Remove the skin and fillet it carefully. Cut into large pieces averaging 1½ inches (4cm). Aim to get at least 24 cubes. (Use off-cuts to make fish soup or stock.)

2 Mix the marinade ingredients together then immerse the fish cubes in it, leaving for up to 2 hours.

3 Preheat the grill to medium, and put the rack on the lowest level. Thread the fish on to four skewers. Ensure the cubes are well coated with marinade, pouring excess over them.

4 Grill (or barbecue) for 10 minutes, turning once or twice.

5 During stage 4, mix the dip ingredients together. Serve, dipping the hot unskewered cubes of fish into the cold dip.

BALIKLAR PLAKI

Mullet casserole

Plaki cooking originated in the Byzantine era centuries ago, and is still widely used in Greece, Turkey and Armenia. Fish or vegetables are baked in olive oil with garlic, herbs and tomato. Traditionally the fish would simply be chopped up and added to the other ingredients, head, tail, skin, bones and all, and fish devotees may prefer that. Personally, I prefer to skin and fillet the fish first. Mullet, grey or red, is often used for this dish, but any fish is equally suitable.

Serves 4

1½lb (675g) grey or red mullet, weighed after stage 1
6 tablespoons olive oil
2 teaspoons paprika
8oz (225g) onion, cut into rings
½ pint (300ml) fish stock or water
4oz (110g) carrot, thinly sliced

3 or 4 sticks celery, diced into ½ inch (1cm) pieces
6 canned plum tomatoes, chopped
4–8 cloves garlic
4 bay leaves
salt and pepper

1 Prepare the fish. Skin and bone it and cut into pieces averaging 2½ inches (6 cm).

2 Heat the olive oil in a casserole dish. Stir-fry the paprika and onion rings for 5 minutes. Add the fish stock or water and, when simmering, the carrot, celery, tomato, garlic cloves and bay leaves.

3 Simmer on the stove for about 20 minutes, allowing the liquid to reduce by one-third. Season with salt and pepper.

4 Preheat the oven to 375°F/190°C/Gas 5 and mix the fish into the casserole. Place in the oven, uncovered, and cook for 20 minutes. Inspect, test for tenderness – it will probably require about 10 minutes more. Add a little water if it is getting too dry.

A favourite Armenian version of this dish uses mackerel and is called *uskumru plaki*.

SARDALYA TAVASI

Pan-fried sardines

The simplest things are often the best and fried sardines are one of those things. Found at all Middle Eastern coastal towns, they sizzle away on racks over charcoal or in frying pans. This particular Turkish recipe uses a shallow griddle pan, a *tava*, and makes a great starter or mezzeh dish. Choose sardines of about 2 oz (50 g) each and about 4 inches (10 cm) long, and serve two per person for a starter. If the fish are smaller than that allow around 4 oz (110 g) per person. This recipe is also ideal for tiny fish such as sprats, whitebait and anchovy, which, when cooked this way, are called *hamsi tavasi*.

Serves 4

8 whole sardines, each weighing   plain white flour
   2oz (50g)   salt
sunflower or light oil   lemon slices

1 Wash the fish and pat dry.
2 Heat some oil in a large frying pan.
3 Dab half the fish in flour and put them into the pan. Stir-fry for about 10 minutes, turning them over and adding oil as necessary.
4 Keep the first fish warm while you cook the remainder.
5 Sprinkle with salt and serve hot with a twist of lemon.

NACHBOUS

Spicy fried shrimps

The seafood which is fished from the Persian Gulf is of outstanding quality, as are the recipes for cooking it. *Nachbous* is a particularly delicious fried shrimp recipe which is found in Kuwait, Bahrain and Saudi Arabia. It uses curry spices and is usually slowly cooked with rice; in this version, the shrimps are cooked separately and served *with* rice.

Serves 4

2lb (900g) brown shrimps,
   crevettes or prawns (200–300 to
   the lb/450g), weighed after
   stage 1
6 tablespoons smen or vegetable
   oil
4–8 cloves garlic, very finely
   chopped
8oz (225g) onions, very finely
   chopped

2 tablespoons finely chopped fresh
   coriander
aromatic salt to taste

SPICES
1 teaspoon baharat
$\frac{1}{2}$ teaspoon turmeric
1 teaspoon ground cummin
1 teaspoon mild curry powder
0–2 teaspoons chilli powder

1 Shell and wash the shrimps, and de-vein them if necessary. If frozen, thaw them in a strainer.

2 Mix the spices in a bowl with enough water to make a paste of pouring consistency. Set aside for a few minutes.

3 Heat the *smen* or oil in a wok or deep frying pan. Stir-fry the garlic for 1 minute then add the spice paste and stir-fry for 2 or 3 minutes. Add the onion and carry on stir-frying for about 10 more minutes.

4 Add the shrimps and coriander and bring to the simmer for 15 minutes. Add a little water if the shrimps are dry and they stick. Stir from time to time and salt to taste.

5 Serve with plain rice (or mix it *into* the rice) and *khoubiz* bread.

GEFILTE

Fish balls

Wherever there is a Jewish community, there is sure to be *gefilte*. They are small balls of ground fish, deep-fried or boiled, and served as a main-course meal with rice and vegetables or as a hot or cold starter. There are a number of recipes for *gefilte* in Israel. This one is typical.

Serves 4

1$\frac{1}{2}$lb (675g) flesh of a white fish
   such as cod or haddock,
   weighed after stage 1
4oz (110g) onions, chopped

2 eggs
2oz (50g) breadcrumbs
salt and pepper to taste

112

1 Prepare the fish. Skin and bone it, and cut into pieces to fit the mincer.

2 Put all the ingredients through a fine mincer or blend in a food processor to achieve a sticky paste texture.

3 Divide the mixture into four then sub-divide each quarter into four, six or eight balls, depending on the size you want.

4 Heat deep-fryer to 375°F/190°C (chip-cooking temperature). Put the balls into the oil, one by one, until half are in the fryer, then cook for 7–8 minutes. Remove them and keep them warm while you do the second batch. Serve cold as a snack or hot with French fries and a twist of lemon.

There are two variants of this recipe. The Turkish version *baliklar koftesi* can be made from the above recipe. Add to the ingredients 1 teaspoon paprika, $\frac{1}{2}$ teaspoon ground cummin and $\frac{1}{2}$ teaspoon ground allspice. The Arab version *blehat samak* can be made from the Turkish version with the addition of 1 teaspoon garlic powder and 1 teaspoon chopped fresh coriander. Shape them into fish fingers.

KESKSHEH BIL HOUT

Fish couscous

This is usually cooked by putting the entire fish into the bottom part of a couscous double steamer. This produces a tasty but rather bony, scaly, mushy mixture of fishy food, much adored by those accustomed to it. I prefer this Libyan method where fish fillets are used. To cook the couscous see page 142. (You can, of course, serve the fish with rice as an alternative.)

Serves 4

1 recipe couscous (page 142)
1½lb (675g) white fish (John Dory or plaice are excellent), weighed after stage 1
8oz (225g) smoked haddock, cut into small pieces, complete with skin
4 bay leaves
8oz (225 g) onions, chopped
4 cloves garlic
2 carrots, diced

2 sticks celery, diced
4 canned tomatoes, chopped
½ teaspoon whole black peppercorns
1 teaspoon ground cummin
1 teaspoon bahar
2 tablespoons smen
20 saffron strands
1 tablespoon chopped fresh coriander
salt

113

1 Prepare the fish. Remove skin, heads and bones and reserve. Cut the flesh into large chunks and set aside.

2 Boil 1½ pints (900 ml) water and put the fish heads, tails, skin and bones into it along with the smoked haddock and bay leaves. Simmer for 1 hour. Strain. Discard the solids and return the liquid to the pan and re-simmer.

3 Add the onion, garlic, carrot, celery, tomatoes, peppercorns, cummin, *bahar* and the *smen*. Simmer for 30–40 minutes.

4 Add the chunks of fish and continue to simmer for about 10 more minutes.

5 Finally drop in the saffron and fresh coriander, and salt to taste. Serve after 5 more minutes' simmering.

CHERMOULA SAMAK

Spicy marinated grilled trout

Chermoula is a spicy coating or marinating paste from Morocco. It is widely used with meat dishes. In this recipe the paste is rubbed into fish steaks, the fish is left to marinate. Sea fish such as sea bass or bream would normally be used, but I find freshwater trout works perfectly.

Serves 4

4 fresh trout, about 12oz (350g)
  each
1 recipe chermoula marinade (see
  page 34)

1 Gut the trout, keeping them in one piece. Carefully wash and dry them.

2 Cut each trout into four pieces then immerse the pieces in the marinade in a large non-metal bowl.

3 Cover the bowl and put it in the fridge for a minimum of 6 and a maximum of 24 hours.

4 Pre-heat the grill to medium hot. Put the rack at its lowest level.

5 Put the fish on to the grill-pan tray and grill for 10–15 minutes, turning twice.

ISTAKOZ FIRINDA

Baked lobster

Lobster is a luxury in all countries, but this subtle Turkish recipe does more than justice to the succulent creatures so readily available in the Istanbul fish market.

Serves 4

4 lobsters or crawfish, about 1lb (450g) each
3 tablespoons vegetable oil
2 cloves garlic, finely chopped
4oz (110g) onions, finely chopped
1 teaspoon paprika
1 tablespoon finely chopped parsley

1 teaspoon finely chopped dill
5fl oz (150ml) soured cream or cream cheese
1 teaspoon cornflour
salt to taste
a little chopped fresh coriander

1 Boil fresh lobsters for 15 minutes and cool. If frozen, thaw. Cleave the shells in two and pick out all the flesh. Discard the long black vein running from tail to head and the stomach sac which is in the head. The remaining flesh, including that in the claws, the bluish liver and any roe, is edible. Chop it into bite-sized pieces. Keep the shells.

2 Heat the oil and stir-fry the garlic and onion for 3 minutes or so. Add the paprika, parsley and dill, with the soured cream or cream cheese and cornflour, and stir briskly, adding a little water until it stops thickening. Salt to taste then add the lobster meat, stirring for 2 or 3 minutes.

3 Pre-heat the oven to 325°F/160°C/Gas 3. Carefully fill the lobster shells with the meat mixture, and put them on two oven trays. Bake for 10–15 minutes.

4 Garnish with coriander, and serve with a rice dish.

SAMAK BIL TAHINE

Cod baked with tahine

This classic Lebanese fish dish is baked in the sesame seed paste, tahine. Traditionally and deliciously, it is served with tabouleh salad and *taratoor b'snorbeh*, a pine nut dip. You can use any fish of your choice with or without heads, skin and bone, but I prefer to use cod fillet steak to give the chunky texture that the dish requires.

Serves 4

1½lb (675g) cod fillet steak	2 tablespoons tahine paste
3 tablespoons olive oil	aromatic salt to taste
2–4 cloves garlic, finely chopped	lemon wedges
4oz (110g) onions, finely chopped	1 tablespoon finely chopped fresh
1 tablespoon dried mint	coriander
½ pint (300ml) milk	

1 Skin the fish and check that all the bones have been removed. Cut into 1½ inch (4cm) cubes.

2 Heat the oil and stir-fry the garlic and onion for 10 minutes. Add the mint, milk and tahine and mix well.

3 Pre-heat the oven to 375°F/190°C/Gas 5, and place the fish in an oven tray.

4 Coat the fish with the fried mixture, adding salt to taste, and bake for about 20 minutes.

5 Garnish with lemon wedges and fresh coriander.

MASGOUF BAGHDADI

Baked curried salmon or sea trout

As far as I can tell this dish is special to Iraq. The fish they use is a freshwater fish called *shabbat*, a kind of salmon or trout. The recipe comes from a new, very luxurious hotel – the Regency – in neighbouring Kuwait, whose 60-chef kitchen is renowned for its cooking. In their description of the dish, the hotel attributed it to Iraq's capital city, Baghdad.

Serves 4

1 whole sea trout, weighing 3lb
  (1·3kg), or 1 middle-cut piece of
  salmon, weighing around 2lb
  (900g)
6–8 cloves garlic, peeled
1 inch (2·5cm) cube ginger, peeled
8oz (225g) onion, peeled
6 tablespoons smen or vegetable oil
6 canned plum tomatoes, chopped
aromatic salt to taste
olive oil for final basting

SPICES (ALL GROUND)
2 teaspoons cummin
1 teaspoon baharat
1 teaspoon cinnamon
1 teaspoon coriander
1 teaspoon black mustard seed
½ teaspoon caraway
½ teaspoon green cardamom
½ teaspoon fenugreek seed

GARNISH
lemon wedges
fresh fennel and coriander leaves

1 Wash the fish, dry and cut small diagonal slashes in the flesh to allow the coating to penetrate.

2 Mix the ground spices together with enough water to make a paste of pouring consistency. Set aside to blend.

3 Put the garlic, ginger and onion into a liquidizer or food processor and purée.

4 Heat the *smen* or oil, and stir-fry the purée for 10 minutes. Add the spice paste and stir-fry for a further 5 minutes. Add the tomatoes and salt to taste.

5 Pre-heat oven to 275°F/140°C/Gas 1. Line one or two oven trays with aluminium foil to prevent the fish sticking. Put the fish on the tray(s), and cover with the fried mixture, working the fish into it. Cover with foil, and bake for 1½ hours.

6 Pre-heat the grill to three-quarters heat. Remove the fish from the oven, and discard the top foil. The fish should be cooked and fairly dry. Baste it with a little olive oil, then put under the grill for 2–3 minutes until it crisps up. Serve with rice and dips.

MAHI NOW ROOZ

Stuffed monkfish

There is a thriving fishing industry in Iran, and a corresponding selection of fish recipes to match. On one traditional occasion each year, fish is eaten throughout Iran, at their New Year (*Now Rooz*), celebrated on the 21st of March, the first day of spring.

This stuffed fish recipe is good at any time of year. It works with any plump, firm fish, but my personal preference is monkfish. Its head is warted, whiskered and so ugly, with its vast red-lipped, spiky-toothed mouth, that it is almost always sold headless and skinned. But its flesh is amazingly tasty, resembling that of lobster or king prawns, and is ideal for stuffing too, having a deep round pocket if carefully boned. For a traditional Persian New Year's meal (great for a dinner party), serve with *chellow, kookoo sabzi, sabzi isfahan khodran,* yoghurt and *torshi* (see pages 148, 139, 57, 38 and 42.)

Serves 4

*1 monkfish tail, about 1–1½lb
(450–675g), weighed after
stage 1*

STUFFING MIXTURE
*1lb (450g) fresh spinach, washed
and finely shredded
4 tablespoons smen or vegetable
oil
4oz (110g) onions, finely chopped
2 tablespoons brown sugar
1 tablespoon sultanas
8 dates, seeded and chopped
6 cherry tomatoes, quartered
1 loomi (dried lime), quartered
1 teaspoon zereshk (dried
barberries)*

*1 tablespoon chopped almonds
1 tablespoon chopped walnuts
1 tablespoon chopped pistachio
nuts
½ teaspoon aromatic salt*

COATING MIXTURE
*5oz (150g) plain yoghurt
2 tablespoons tomato ketchup
2–4 cloves garlic, finely chopped
1 teaspoon turmeric
1 teaspoon powdered cinnamon
2 tablespoons walnut oil*

GARNISH
*fresh or dried mint
lime wedges*

1 Prepare the fish. Carefully bone it, leaving a pouch to hold the stuffing. Wash it and pat dry.

2 Start the stuffing mixture. Blanch the spinach for 2 minutes. Strain and set aside. At the same time, prepare the coating mixture, whisking the ingredients together with a fork. Set aside.

3 Heat the *smen* or oil for the stuffing and stir-fry the onion for about 5 minutes. Add the sugar and when it melts, add the other stuffing ingredients including the spinach. Stir to the simmer to blend and soften it. Set aside to cool enough to work with.

4 Preheat the oven to 375°F/190°C/Gas 5. Put aluminium foil on to an oven tray to prevent the fish sticking. Carefully stuff the fish, but don't *over*stuff. Try to enclose the stuffing, and keep any spare aside.

5 Place the fish on to the oven tray and baste it with one-third of the coating mixture.

6 Bake in the oven for 20 minutes. Turn the fish over, baste with another third of the coating mixture, and bake for a further 20 minutes.

7 Turn it again and baste with the remaining coating mixture and bake for 10–20 minutes more.

8 Garnish with fresh or dried mint and lime wedges.

CHAPTER 9

VEGETABLE AND EGG DISHES

A S WE have seen, the cooking of the Middle East has its roots back in the mists of time. Early civilized man had to hand a very wide selection of vegetables growing indigenously, and soon these were being cultivated and cooked in all manner of interesting ways. These vegetables included aubergine (*badenjan*), beet (*bangar*), broad beans (*ful*), cabbage (*kharoom malfouf*), carrots (*jazar*), cauliflower (*arnabit*), courgettes/zucchini (*kossa*), cucumber (*khiyar*), garlic (*tum*), globe artichokes (*kharshoof*), grape-vine leaves (*warak-einab*), leeks (*korrat*), lettuce (*khass*), marrow (*kossa*), *melokhia*, mushrooms (*fou-oh*), okra (*bamiya*), olives (*zaytun*), onions (*basal*), peas (*baseeh*), spinach (*sabanek*) and turnips (*lift*).

In addition, the early farmers soon learned that the seeds of plants of the legume family were edible and could be eaten fresh, but more importantly, they could be dried. This discovery enabled stores of beans (*fassoolia*), lentils (*ads*) and chickpeas (*houmous*) to be built up for winters and famines. These ingredients gave rise to a wealth of great dishes, some of them created thousands of years ago and still the backbone of today's Middle Eastern cooking. I have included several such ancient and traditional dishes in this chapter. But the observant will notice that many familiar vegetables are missing. These include the avocado, capsicum pepper (*filfil akhdar*), chilli pepper (*filfil shattah*), French beans (*fassoolia khadra*), Jerusalem artichokes (*tartoufa*), maize (*durra*), plantains (*moz*), potato (*batata*), tomato (*bandora*) and celery (*karafs*). All of these were discovered in the 'New World' in the sixteenth century (along with chocolate, peanuts, tobacco, turkeys and vanilla). These 'new' vegetables soon arrived in the 'Old World', and are now an inextricable part of Middle Eastern cooking. Many of the recipes in this chapter feature them.

Also in this chapter are recipes for egg dishes, the celebrated stuffed vine-leaf dish, *dolmas*, and an intriguing noodle dish. I should mention finally that it is very common for meat to be cooked with vegetable dishes in Middle Eastern cooking. Naturally, all the recipes in this chapter are meat-free.

MELOKHIA

Green vegetables

Melokhia is a green leafy vegetable that has been grown in Egypt for thousands of years. It is a little like spinach in colour and texture, with oval leaves growing on long stalks, but it is considerably smaller, the average leaf being about 3 inches (7·5cm). It is available at Covent Garden on a regular basis between May and September, and a good greengrocers could get it for you then. Failing that, it is available frozen from specialist shops, and dried.

The *melokhia* is normally chopped very finely with a *makhrata*, a sharp crescent-shaped, two-handled blade (identical to the *mezzaluna* used in the West) by rotating it over the vegetables. The other method is harder but more elegant, and requires the leaves to be 'shaved' into long, very thin strips, like Chinese seaweed. Use a cleaver to achieve this.

Serves 4

1½lb (675g) fresh melokhia leaves,
weighed after stage 1, or frozen,
or 6oz (175g) dry melokhia plus
1¼lb (550g) fresh spinach leaves,
weighed after stage 1
4–8 cloves garlic, finely chopped

8oz (225g) onions, chopped
6–8 bay leaves
6–8 green cardamoms
2–4 teaspoons ground coriander
6 canned tomatoes (optional)
some ta'leyah (see page 53)

1 Prepare the leaves. Cut away and discard stalks. Chop as described above.

2 Bring ¾ pint (450ml) water (or chicken stock) to the boil, and add all the ingredients except the *melokhia* and *ta'leyah*. Simmer for 1 hour.

3 Blanch the leaves in a separate pan of boiling water for a couple of minutes. Strain and add to the simmering pan. Mix well and serve as soon as the leaves are cooked to your liking.

4 Garnish with the *ta'leyah*.

LATKES

Shredded potato cakes

These are delicious fried rissoles, enjoyed by Jewish communities the world over, at all times of the year, but particularly to celebrate Jewish religious festivals. I will never forget the first encounter I had with latkes. I was in a New York yellow cab and its driver was a little, fat, talkative Jew from the Bronx. I was intending to travel down town from 54th Street on a journey of about twenty blocks, which should have taken about 10 minutes. When he realized I was English he decided to tell me about New York, with the non-stop patter of virtually all taxi drivers, while stuffing his face with something golden in colour. Suddenly he offered me one. 'Mama' (his wife) cooked it the day before, he said, advising me that it was a latke. I asked him where in New York I could get them. The upshot was that he turned the meter off, after ensuring that I had time to spare, and whisked me off to a taxi drivers' Jewish café on Orchard Street by Manhattan Bridge. The street outside was treble parked with yellow cabs and police cars, and the café was seething with their drivers. I got my latkes and spent a most enjoyable hour. Latkes are now very much an Israeli dish.

Serves 4 (12 latkes)

1lb (450g) potatoes	*½ teaspoon ground white pepper*
8oz (225g) onions, finely chopped	*½ teaspoon salt*
1 egg	*1 teaspoon white sugar*
1 tablespoon cornflour	*vegetable oil for frying*
6oz (175g) plain flour	

1 Scrub and peel the potatoes, then cut into julienne or grate (by hand or by machine, pulsing carefully or else it goes mushy. Rinse in cold water to remove starch.

2 Mix all the ingredients together (except the oil, which you heat in a large flat frying pan) with sufficient water to form a stiffish paste.

3 Divide the mixture into twelve, then press each into an oval shape about 3½ inches (8cm) long. Fry them four at a time, turning two or three times until golden brown. Serve with pastrami and bagels.

KOSSA MASHIYA BIL KIBBEH

Courgettes (zucchini) stuffed with kibbeh

Courgettes look especially attractive when stuffed, and this Lebanese recipe uses a *kibbeh* mixture (see page 82) or, for a non-meat alternative, burghul. The success of the dish depends on using smallish courgettes, and on coring them neatly. Special corers called *ma'wara* with sharp tips range from $\frac{1}{4}$ inch (6mm) to about 1 inch (2·5cm). The latter is about the size of an apple corer, which is a little too large for courgettes. The ideal size is about $\frac{3}{4}$ inch (2cm), but as *ma'wara* are difficult to obtain, I used a very slim knife to cut with and a cigar tube with which to push the filling out.

Serves 4

16 courgettes, each about 3 inches (7·5cm) long
4 tablespoons vegetable oil

2oz (50g) onions, finely chopped
$\frac{1}{2}$ recipe kibbeh (see page 82)
1 teaspoon baharat

1 Wash the courgettes then cut off the tops and tails. Carefully remove the centre core (retaining it for future use), as described above. Leave about $\frac{1}{4}$ inch (6mm) of skin and flesh all round, and don't pierce the skin or it will probably split during cooking.

2 Heat the oil and stir-fry the onion, *kibbeh* or burghul and *baharat* for 7 or 8 minutes. Strain and let cool, while the oven pre-heats to 325°F/160°C/Gas 3.

3 Carefully stuff the courgettes with the cool mixture and line them up side by side on an oven tray.

4 Bake for 15 minutes.

The Saudi version of this dish is called *sheik-el-ma'shi*.

KABAK MUCVER

Courgette fritters

I have included this Turkish recipe because it solves the problem of what to do with the cores of the courgettes from the previous recipe. The answer is to freeze them until you come to make this.

Serves 4 (8 fritters)

the cores from 16 courgettes, mashed
4 tablespoons cornflour
4 tablespoons plain white flour
aromatic salt and pepper to taste
2 eggs
8oz (225g) onions, chopped

2 cloves garlic, finely chopped
3oz (75g) Cheddar or feta cheese, grated
2 tablespoons chopped fresh coriander
5floz (150ml) vegetable oil

1 Put the cornflour and plain flour in a bowl and add just enough water to make a thickish paste. Season to taste and beat in the eggs.

2 Mix in all the remaining ingredients, except for the oil.

3 Heat the oil in a large flat frying pan. Spoon out a dollop of about an eighth of the mixture, and place it in the pan. Press it down with the back of the spoon to create a thick disc shape. Repeat with three more.

4 Fry these four discs, turning once or twice, until golden (about 8–10 minutes).

5 Repeat with the remainder of the mixture.

YERELMASI ZEYTINYAGLI

Jerusalem artichoke cooked in olive oil

The Jerusalem artichoke is a tuber with a sweet and nutty taste. Originally from North America, it is not related to globe artichokes, being a species of sunflower, and has nothing to do with Jerusalem either, having gained its name from the Italian word for sunflower, *girasole*. This Turkish recipe simmers the artichoke with carrot, celery and rice.

Serves 4

12oz (350g) Jerusalem artichokes, weighed after stage 1	3 tablespoons dry basmati rice
4 tablespoons olive oil	6floz (175ml) vegetable stock or water
4oz (110g) onions, chopped	salt to taste
4oz (110g) carrots, scraped and thinly sliced	1 lemon
4oz (110g) celery, chopped	sprinkling chopped parsley

1 Pare the artichokes and remove knobbles and scars in much the same way as for ginger. Immediately cut into $\frac{1}{2}$ inch (1cm) cubes, and keep in cold water to prevent discolouring.

2 Heat the oil, and stir-fry the onion for 5 minutes. Strain the artichokes and add them, the carrots, the celery and the rice to the pan.

3 Stir-fry for about 5 minutes then add the vegetable stock or water and bring to the boil. Simmer for about 20 minutes. Add more water if required.

4 Salt to taste and serve with a squeeze of lemon and a sprinkling of parsley.

ENGINAR ZEYTINYAGLI

Globe artichoke

This recipe uses the other artichoke, the globe artichoke, which is a variety of thistle and is indigenous to North Africa. Indeed artichokes are very cheap and plentiful there and appear in salads and *tagines* and stuffed in the recipes of the Maghreb. The globe artichoke is equally popular in Turkey, as this recipe demonstrates.

Serves 4

4 globe artichokes	4oz (110g) carrots, thinly sliced
2 tablespoons vinegar, any type	1 tablespoon sugar
2 tablespoons olive oil	1 teaspoon salt
16 tiny pickling onions, peeled and whole	1 teaspoon black pepper
1 teaspoon powdered cinnamon	1 fresh lemon
4oz (110g) broad beans (frozen and thawed or fresh)	sprinkling of chopped fresh parsley

1 Wash the artichokes under a running cold tap to remove grit. Boil them in water for 15 minutes, then cool to handle.

2 Cut away the leaves and expose base. Cut away the top half. Scoop out the hairy filaments of the choke. Remove the stem from the base then trim the hard outer parts from the base and sides. Put the prepared hearts into a bowl of cold water with the vinegar. This prevents discoloration.

3 Heat the oil in a large saucepan. Stir-fry the whole onions, cinnamon, broad beans and carrots for 10 minutes. Add the artichokes and water to cover, and simmer for about 1 hour. Add further water if it gets too dry.

4 Just before serving, add the sugar and salt and pepper to taste. Garnish with a squeeze of lemon and sprinkling of parsley.

Note: Use the leaves to start a vegetable stock. Simmer for 1 hour then strain and discard them.

BAMIYA B'ZAYT

Stir-fried okra

Okra is the pod of a plant native to Africa. It is green, five-sided and chilli-shaped, with a pointed end, and is called 'ladies finger'. Okra has always been an important vegetable in the Middle Eastern repertoire. The traditional way of cooking okra, or *bamiya*, is to stew it for half an hour or so until sappy and sticky. Personally, I find this texture not to my taste, and prefer a crunchy okra. This Lebanese method uses a quick stir-fry technique which retains all the delicate flavours.

Serves 4 as a main course

8 tablespoons olive oil
4–8 cloves garlic, finely chopped
1 tablespoon ground coriander
* seeds*
8oz (225g) onions, chopped
14oz (400g) can plum tomatoes
* and juice*

1½lb (675g) tender fresh okra
1 tablespoon lemon juice
1 tablespoon sugar
1 tablespoon chopped fresh
* coriander*
aromatic salt and black pepper to
* taste*

1 Heat half the oil in a wok or large frying pan. Stir-fry the garlic for 1 minute, then the ground coriander for a further minute. Add the onions and stir-fry for 5 minutes.

2 Now add the tomatoes and their juice and bring to the simmer, stirring from time to time.

3 During stage 2 wash the okra, then dry them. Cut off the pointed tip and the stalk and discard them.

4 Put the contents of the wok into a bowl.

5 Heat the remaining oil and while it is heating cut the okra into 1 inch (2·5cm) pieces, and put them into the wok straightaway. Gently toss for 5 minutes.

6 Add the reserved tomato mixture plus the lemon juice, sugar and fresh coriander. When simmering, season to taste with salt and pepper. Serve at once. (Do not store or freeze this dish as it will go mushy.)

KEREVIZ TEREYAGLI

Sautéed celery

This is one of the simplest vegetable dishes, coming from Turkey as do so many. It is quite delicious. Celery is cooked in butter (*tereyagli*) or alternatively *smen* (*susmeyagli*). An Arab version of this dish is called *karafsi magaali* and it contains *za'atar*.

Serves 4

1½lb (675g) celery, weighed after
    stage 1
3oz (75g) smen or butter

1 tablespoon za'atar (Arabian
    option)
aromatic salt to taste
1 tablespoon lemon juice

1 Wash the celery, discard the thin stalks and leaves, which are usually bitter. Chop the celery into 2 inch (5cm) chunks.

2 Blanch the celery in boiling water for 3–5 minutes, then strain (reserve the water for future stock).

3 Heat the *smen* or butter in a wok. Add the still hot celery and stir-fry for 3 or 4 minutes. Add the remaining ingredients and stir-fry for a further few minutes. Serve hot.

BRAS YAHNI

Sautéed leeks

From Armenia comes this light leek dish. It has a hint of sweetness which, if you wish, can be made more pronounced by adding more sugar. The Saudi version of this dish is called *korrat bi zayt* and it uses a miniature type of leek called *korrat*. Use spring onions in combination with leeks for this version and omit the sugar.

Serves 4

1lb (450g) leeks, weighed after
   stage 1
4 tablespoons vegetable or olive
   oil
2–6 cloves garlic
4 fresh tomatoes, chopped
1–3 tablespoons brown sugar
   (Armenian option)

1 bunch barbeen or watercress,
   chopped
1 bunch spring onions (Saudi
   option)
1–3 teaspoons chilli powder
   (Saudi option)
salt to taste
½ pint (300ml) yahni stock or water

1 Wash the leeks carefully, ensuring no mud, etc, remains between the leaves. Shake dry, then cut off the hairy root ends and any spoiled leaf tips or leaves. Chop into pieces about 1½ inches (4cm) in length.

2 Heat the oil. Stir-fry the garlic for 1 minute, then add all the remaining and optional items except the stock and leeks, stir-frying for 3 minutes.

3 Add the leeks and when sizzling, pour in the *yahni* stock or water. Simmer for 10–15 minutes (it is not critical), stirring occasionally.

CHAKCHOUKA

Ratatouille-style vegetables

The *chakchouka* or *tchoutchouka* is a style of vegetable cooking from the Maghreb. It generally contains garlic and onion fried in olive oil with tomatoes, peppers and a principal vegetable such as courgettes, marrow, aubergine, artichoke, cauliflower, beans, etc. The *chakchouka* can be likened to the Turkish *plaki* or the French *ratatouille*. Very often *chakchouka* dishes are finished by pouring beaten eggs over the dish at the final stages of cooking. This is stated as an option in this spicy Algerian recipe.

Serves 4

3 tablespoons sunflower oil
2 cloves garlic, finely chopped
8oz (225g) onions, chopped
1 red and/or green capsicum
  pepper, chopped
14oz (400g) can tomatoes with
  juice
1lb (450g) courgettes (zucchini)
7oz (200g) can white haricot or
  broad beans with juice
  (optional)

2–6 fresh green or red chillies,
  chopped (optional)
1 teaspoon cummin seeds
  (optional)
2 teaspoons brown sugar
salt
2 eggs (optional)
1 tablespoon finely chopped
  parsley

1 Heat the oil in a wok or large frying pan. Stir-fry the garlic for 1 minute then the onion for about 5 minutes more.

2 Add the peppers and the tomatoes with their juice. Simmer for 10 minutes.

3 During this time prepare the principal vegetable, here courgettes. Wash, top and tail, then cut into 1 inch (2·5cm) pieces and blanch in boiling water for 3 minutes.

4 Strain (reserving water for future stock), and add to the wok along with the haricot or broad beans. Add the optional items and sugar, and simmer for 5 minutes. Salt to taste.

5 If you want this as an eggy version, lightly beat the eggs with a fork, then pour them all over the *chakchouka*. Cook on the stove until the egg sets. Garnish with the parsley and serve hot with *khoubiz* bread or rice.

A Turkish *sebzeler plaki* can be made from the above recipe by omitting the spicy options and egg. And *chakchouka merguez* contains the Maghreb sausage, *merguez* (see page 62). Chop it up and add at the beginning of stage 2.

RIGHT, CLOCKWISE FROM THE TOP: *Khoubiz* (Arab bread) page 153, *Istakoz Firinda* (baked lobster) page 115, *Nachbous* (spicy fried shrimps) page 111, with *Chellow* (Iranian rice) page 148, *Masgouf Baghdadi* (baked curried sea trout) page 116, *Kilich Shish* (skewered swordfish) page 109, with its garlic dip.

FASSOOLIA BAYDAH

White haricot beans

Beans mean *fassoolia* in the Levant, *fasooliya* in Egypt, *fasulyah* in Saudi Arabia, *fasulye* in Turkey and *fassolakia* in Greece. The kind of bean being referred to depends on the suffix: for example, *fassoolia khadra* is fresh runner beans.

Fassoolia baydah is white dry haricot beans. As with many Middle Eastern vegetable dishes, more often than not chunks of meat on the bone are simmered in the pot. This Syrian recipe omits the meat and the resultant white bean dish is attractive and very tasty. Serve as a side dish with meat and bread or rice. Use either pearl haricots, the small white beans, or white haricots, the larger, creamy, flat beans. (Incidentally, pearl haricot beans means Heinz in Britain, for it is these which when canned with tomato sauce become the familiar 'baked beans'.)

Serves 4

9oz (250g) dry haricot beans
4 tablespoons vegetable oil
2–4 cloves garlic, chopped
8oz (225g) onions, chopped
$\frac{1}{2}$ teaspoon ground green
    cardamom
1 teaspoon powdered cinnamon
1 teaspoon chilli powder
    (optional)

$\frac{1}{2}$ teaspoon ground black pepper
6 tomatoes, chopped
$\frac{1}{2}$ pint (300ml) yahni stock or water
salt to taste

GARNISH
twists of lemon
a sprinkle of chopped fresh herbs

1 Pick through the beans to ensure there is no grit, then rinse them in cold water a few times. Put them into a large bowl with plenty of cold water and leave them for between 12 and 24 hours to swell.

2 Next day rinse the beans a few times. Boil 3 or 4 pints (1·75 or 2·3 litres) of water, add the beans and boil for at least an hour, until they are as tender as you want them.

3 Heat the oil. Stir-fry the garlic for 1 minute, then the onion for a further 5 minutes. Add the cardamom, cinnamon, chilli and pepper and stir in well. Then add the tomatoes and the stock or water, and simmer for 5–10 minutes.

4 Add the drained beans. Serve hot, garnished with the lemon and herbs.

LEFT, CLOCKWISE FROM THE TOP: *Biber Tursu* (vinegared chillies) page 43, *Kookoo Sabzi* (herbal omelette) page 139, *Saluf bi Hilbeh* (Yemeni spicy bread) page 154, *Houmous ye Esfenaj* (chickpeas with spinach) page 132, *Bamiya B'zayt* (stir-fried okra) page 125, *Latkes* (shredded potato cakes) page 121, *Limoon Makbous* (pickled lemon) page 44, *Torshi* (pickles) page 42, *Dolmades* (stuffed vine leaves) page 135.

FUL MEDAMIS or EL-FUL

Brown Egyptian beans

This bean dish is always described as Egypt's national dish, and it is astonishingly popular. The Egyptian word *ful* or *fool* means beans, and there are many types. Most popular are *ful roomi*, red kidney beans; *ful haman*, pigeon peas (or gunga peas or *toor dhal*); *ful baladi sa'idi*, white, middle-sized beans; *ful akdar*, green-skinned broad beans; *ful nabed*, brown-skinned broad beans; and *ful medamis*, small, round, brown broad beans with a small black stripe, also called tic, horse, or Egyptian brown beans. Confusion arises with the latter two types because they are both varieties of *fava* bean, and both are white when their brown skins are removed.

Ful cooking is taken very seriously in Egypt and a special cooking pot – the *damassa* or *idra* – is used just for the purpose. It is a vase-shaped metal pan with a narrow neck and tight-fitting lid. It holds a small amount of water and the neck design causes the water to condense and drop back into the pan so that the water will last throughout the cooking time. The recipe below and the one following come from the Felfela restaurant, Hoda Sharawi Street, Cairo, it's really cheap there and is always full of locals enjoying good local dishes. One section of their menu runs to 15 different *ful* dishes ranging from *ful* with oil for £1 to *ful* with *pastruma* and eggs for £3.75.

Serves 4 as a main course

10oz (300g) *ful medamis*
1 recipe *ta'leyah* (see page 53)
1 teaspoon ground cummin
2 tablespoons finely chopped
   parsley

1 teaspoon aromatic salt
2 tablespoons olive oil

GARNISH
lemon wedges

1 Pick through the dry beans, removing grit or withered ones. Rinse, then soak them in a bowl large enough to accommodate the beans as they swell, with 3 times their volume of cold water. Leave for 24 hours in the fridge.

2 Next day, rinse the beans. Bring $1\frac{1}{2}$ times their volume of water to the boil, add the beans and simmer until they are tender but not mushy. Test after 1 hour (cooking times vary depending on the exact type of bean). It is more likely to take 2 or even 3 hours. Add more water if needed, but you don't want too much water in the finished dish, which should have whole beans in a little creamy liquid.

3 Add the remaining ingredients. Garnish with lemon wedges, and serve hot with *aiysh* (see page 155), salads and yoghurt.

FUL NABED

Egyptian broad beans

The same recipe is used to cook these larger beans. After the soaking period squeeze off the brown skins to reveal bright white beans. Follow the remainder of the recipe. They should cook quicker than *ful medamis*. This dish can be served as in the previous recipe. Alternatively, both recipes can be served as soup by puréeing the beans and adding water to the consistency of your choice.

'ADS BI GIBBA

Brown lentils

The Arabic for lentils is *'ads* (*adas* in Iran). The most popular lentils in the Gulf and the Levant are yellow split lentils (*'ads asfar*), which are used in soups and stews, and brown whole lentils with skins (*'ads bi gibba*, literally lentils in a cloak). These local brown lentils, are small, hard, round pellets, which require a long soaking and cooking time, but which retain their shape and are good for soups and sautées as well as stews and soups. A good substitute is the French *puy* lentil.

The imported Indian brown lentil (*masoor dhal*) can be used. Called *'ads iswid*, they are the familiar red (orange) lentils, which have pale brown skins. They tend to go very soft when cooked.

This recipe is from Jordan. A virtually identical Egyptian variation omits the celery but calls for 20 cloves of garlic!

Serves 4

8oz (225g) whole brown lentils
1 recipe ta'leyah (see page 33)
1 teaspoon ground coriander
1 teaspoon cummin seeds
4oz (110g) celery, diced
aromatic salt

GARNISH
2 tablespoons olive oil (optional)
a sprinkling of chopped fresh
  herbs

1 Pick through the lentils to remove grit, etc, then soak them overnight in ample water in a large bowl.

2 Next day rinse them several times, then put them into a pan with $1\frac{1}{2}$ times their volume of water and simmer until tender. (Timing will vary depending on lentil type, so test after 30 minutes and every 10 minutes

after that.) Keep an eye on the water content. Add more if the lentils need it.

3 While the lentils are cooking, make the *ta'leyah*.

4 If there is too much water remaining in the lentils, strain it off (keep for stock), then mix all the ingredients together back in the same pan and simmer for about 10 minutes. (Add in some lentil water if required.)

5 Garnish with the olive oil (optional) and chopped herbs. Serve with rice and/or *khoubiz* bread for a complete and delicious meal.

HOUMOUS YE ESFENAJ
Chickpeas with spinach

Chickpeas (houmous, humus or *h'missa*) originated in the Middle East and are grown abundantly throughout the area, thriving in arid conditions. They can be used fresh, but they are most common dried, when they are milled into flour, coarsely ground for *houmous b'tahine* (see page 46) and used whole as in this recipe. White chickpeas are used (black or red varieties also exist), and they must be soaked for 12–18 hours to enable them to soften and swell.

This combination of golden chickpeas interspersed with dark green strips of spinach is delightful in appearance as well as taste, and is found virtually identical in all countries. It is *h'missa bil selg* (Maghreb), *humus wa sabanekh* (Egypt), *houmous bi sabanik* (Levant and the Gulf), *nohout ispanakli* (Turkey) and *siserov sbanakh* or *nivig* (Armenia). This is an Iranian version.

Serves 4

12oz (375g) chickpeas
3 tablespoons vegetable oil
2–4 cloves garlic, chopped
4oz (110g) onion, chopped
½–2 tablespoons harissa
  (Maghrebi option)
1 tablespoon cummin seeds,
  roasted (Egyptian option)
2 teaspoons baharat (Saudi
  option)
1 tablespoon brown sugar (Iranian
  and Armenian option)

2 teaspoons powdered cinnamon
  (Iranian and Turkish option)
4–6 canned tomatoes, plus juice
1lb (450g) spinach, finely sliced
aromatic salt and black pepper to
  taste

GARNISH
2 tablespoons smen or olive oil
1 tablespoon fresh lemon juice
a sprinkling of chopped fresh
  herbs

1 Pick through the chickpeas for pieces of grit. (Chickpeas are traditionally spread out on flat rooftops and dried in the sun which is why grit is commonly found in packets.)

2 Rinse them, then soak in plenty of cold water in a large bowl. Leave overnight, or for between 12 and 18 hours.

3 Strain, rinse then boil in a pan containing 4 or 5 pints (2·5–3 litres) water. Cook for 45–60 minutes.

4 Meanwhile, prepare the sauce and spinach. Heat the oil and stir-fry the garlic for 1 minute, then the onion for 5–6 minutes. Add some or all of the options to your taste at this stage, and stir-fry for 2 more minutes. Add the tomatoes and juice and bring to a simmer.

5 During stage 4, bring a further largish pan of water to the boil (about 2 pints/1 litre). Immerse the shredded spinach in it and simmer for 4–5 minutes. Strain.

6 As soon as the chickpeas are cooked to the tenderness of your choice, strain them, discarding the water. Either cool and freeze them (see note below) or, using the same pan, combine the stir-fry mixture, spinach and chickpeas, and bring to the simmer. Add salt and pepper to taste.

7 Place in a serving bowl, garnishing with curls of melted *smen* or olive oil, lemon juice and herbs. Serve with *khoubiz* bread or rice, salad and pickles for a satisfying meal.

Note: Most chickpeas come in 500g packets often originating in India (where they are called *kabli chana*). I usually use two packets and, when cooked and cooled, open-freeze them on a tray before storing the loose peas in freezer bags.

NOKHOD

Lentils, chickpeas and spinach

A variation popular in the northern Levant and with the Kurdish peoples of western Iran, uses a 50:50 mixture of brown lentils and chickpeas, and is prepared in exactly the same way as the previous recipe.

BATATEH MA'LI BIL FELFEL SUDANI

French fries with spicy sauce

I have no idea whether this dish is authentic and where its place in history is. I suspect it is modern, and the invention of the place where I ate it. I don't think that matters, as it is delicious, and as much a part of the Middle East as are any other recipes in this book. This one comes from Morocco. I encountered it, as they say in the movies, 'on the road to Marrakesh'. The city was ahead, a lush festoon of green set in a dusty plain, framed by the high snowy peaks of the Atlas mountains behind it. The waterhole was a nondescript roadside café. The meal on offer was sausage and chips with red sauce. What the heck? I was hungry. I did not expect a gastronomic experience. It just goes to show how wrong one can be. These were indeed chips, but they were deep fried in olive oil and saturated with fresh lemon juice. The sausage was *merguez* (see page 62) and the red sauce was home-made, hot and spicy. *Felfel sudani* is the Moroccan version of harissa.

Serves 4

1–1½lb (450–675g) potatoes, quantity determined by the amount you want to eat	a sprinkling of aromatic salt
	juice of 2 lemons
	1 recipe harissa (see page 51)
2 pints (1·1 litres) olive oil	merguez (see page 62) optional

1 Wash, peel and chop the potatoes to chip size. Leave them in cold water for 1 hour to reduce the starch content. Rinse and dry in kitchen paper.

2 Pre-heat the oil in a deep-fryer or saucepan to 375°F/190°C, then deep-fry half the potatoes for about 6 minutes until they are pale gold. Remove from the oil. Allow the fat temperature to get back to 375°F/190°C, and repeat with the other half. It does not matter if they cool down.

3 Prepare the harissa, and heat it and the accompanying *merguez*.

4 Just before you intend to serve up, ensure the oil is at the correct temperature, then fry the chips again for a couple of minutes. Remove from the oil, and place on kitchen paper to degrease. Drench with lemon juice and serve at once.

DOLMADES

Stuffed vine leaves

All the countries of the Middle East have their *dolma* items, which are very ancient, traceable back to before 1000 BC, at the time of the Hittite Empire. Literally, *dolma* means 'to stuff' (vegetables), and any suitable vegetable would have been stuffed then – artichokes, marrows, courgettes, cabbage leaves and, more latterly, potatoes, tomatoes and peppers. But by far the most popular 'vegetable' for stuffing was and still is the grape vine leaf. Known as dolmades or *dolmathakia* in Greece, as *yaprakh dolmasi* in Turkey, *derevi sarma* or *dolma* in Armenia, *dolmeh-ye barge* in Iran, as *wara-einab mishi* in the Levant and as *malfouf* in the Gulf, the stuffings can include rice, meat, fish, burghul and lentils.

The leaves themselves can occasionally be obtained fresh in Britain, but they are widely distributed in vacuum packs.

The dolmades are traditionally simmered on a stove in a heavy pan, and the water quantity is absorbed by the dolmades. To prevent them sticking and tearing when lifted out, the inside of the pan is lined with torn or excess vine leaves. The oven method is unconventional but easier.

Makes 24 dolmades

30 *vine leaves (to allow for breakages)*
olive oil

STUFFING
4oz (110g) *cooked and cooled rice*
2oz (50g) *onions, chopped and fried*
2oz (50g) *pine nuts, roasted and chopped*

1 tablespoon *chopped fresh mint*
1 tablespoon *sultanas and/or dates, chopped (optional)*
1 tablespoon *tomato ketchup*
1 teaspoon *bahar*
$\frac{1}{2}$ teaspoon *aromatic salt*
1 teaspoon *white sugar*

1 Mix the stuffing ingredients together. It should be cold and sticky enough to shape, and is enough for 24 vine leaves.

2 If the leaves are fresh, de-stalk and wash them. Then blanch them in boiling water for 15 seconds. Strain and allow to cool. If the leaves are vacuum-packed, you will need to wash out the brine in several cold water rinses.

3 Spread the vine leaf flat on a work surface. Put a dollop of filling on to it and roll to produce a cylinder about $2 \times \frac{3}{4}$ inches (5×2cm) as shown in the diagram.

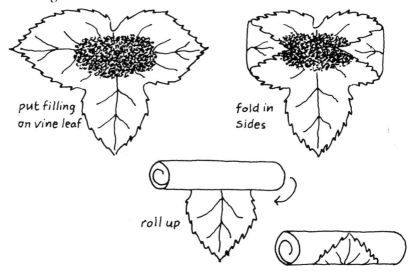

put filling
on vine leaf

fold in
sides

roll up

4 To prevent the vine leaves sticking during cooking use a non-stick pastry oven tray. If you don't have such a tray, line an ordinary one with cling film (it won't melt). Brush the tray (or film) with olive oil. Place the dolmades on it with the tip of the rolled leaf downwards. Do not squash them, just let them touch each other lightly. Brush them with olive oil, and cover the tray(s) with aluminium foil. Put into the oven preheated to 300°F/150°C/Gas 2, and cook for 20–30 minutes. Serve hot or cold.

TUTMAJ

Noodles with yoghurt

Pasta is always considered to be Italian (the very word pasta is Latin for paste), but it was thought to be the Chinese who invented it in the form of noodles over 6,000 years ago. Noodles and noodle-making methods filtered from China via the trade routes, most probably by the first century AD when the 'Silk Route' to China was first established, at which time the entire Mediterranean was under Roman control. With Roman decline, pasta expertise centred in Italy, but isolated pockets of noodle makers remained – in particular in Turkey and Armenia. Today's Middle East enjoys all forms of pasta Italian style just as much as everyone else, and pizza/pasta bars vie with kebab houses in most Arab cities. But *tutmaj* is different. It is normally served as a soup, but it is delicious as a thick gravied vegetable dish.

Serves 4

*1lb (450g) fresh egg noodles or 1lb
(450g) tagliatelli*
*2 tablespoons sunflower or soya
oil*
4oz (110g) onions, chopped
2 cloves garlic, chopped (optional)
*4floz (100ml) vegetable stock or
water*

5oz (150g) thick Greek yoghurt
1 tablespoon cornflour
1 egg
20 strands saffron (optional)
salt to taste
*a sprinkling of chopped mint and
parsley*

1 Bring 3 pints (1·75 litres) water to the boil in a large saucepan. Immerse the noodles or tagliatelli and simmer for 5–10 minutes. Stir from time to time, and test to get exactly the texture you like. Strain.

2 During stage 1 heat the oil, and stir-fry the onion and garlic for 5 minutes.

3 During stage 2, whisk together the vegetable stock, yoghurt, cornflour, egg and saffron.

4 Remove the stir-fry from the heat and add the yoghurt mixture, stirring it in fast. Return to the heat, stir all the time and the yoghurt should not curdle as it is heated.

5 Once it starts to simmer, add the noodles and mix well. Add salt and fresh mint and parsley to taste, and serve on its own or to accompany a meat dish.

Note: If you want it as a soup add more stock or water at stage 3.

YOGURTLU PAPYON MAKARNA

A Turkish variation of *tutmaj* replaces the noodles with bow-tie pasta (*fiochetti*), which are available plain or green. Simply substitute one for the other and follow the previous recipe.

MENEMEN

Scrambled egg with peppers

Simple, effective and deliciously tasty, this Turkish recipe can serve as a snack, light meal or an accompaniment dish. The quantities here will give an ample amount for four. Scale quantities down as required.

Serves 4 as a main dish

1 red capsicum pepper	8 cherry tomatoes
1 green capsicum pepper	8 eggs
2–4 fresh chillies (optional)	aromatic salt and black pepper
1 tablespoon olive oil	a sprinkling of chopped fresh
2 cloves garlic, chopped	coriander

1 Chop the red and green peppers into small diamond shapes discarding seeds and pith. Chop the chillies into thin rings.

2 Heat the oil and stir-fry the garlic for 1 minute. Add the peppers and chillies and a splash of water to prevent them sticking, and stir-fry for 5 minutes or so. Add another splash of water and the whole tomatoes, and carefully stir-fry to soften but not split them.

3 Beat the eggs lightly with a fork, then pour them over the stir-fry mixture. Reduce heat. Allow the eggs to start to set, then stir carefully until it is ready to serve. Watch that it doesn't burn and stick.

4 Garnish with salt, pepper and fresh coriander. Serve with pitta bread or toast.

Kookoo Sabzi

Herbal omelette

It is slightly misleading to call this celebrated Iranian dish an omelette, because it is quite thick and firmly set and packed with green herbs, quite unlike the very light, thin, folded Western omelette. The *kookoo* has many filling variations including vegetables, potatoes and meat.

Of all the variations *kookoo sabzi* is probably Iran's favourite. The best way to get the texture right is to bake it in a round flan tray in the oven. Serve it as a light meal or to accompany other dishes.

The Arabian version of this dish is called *ijjah bil tawabel*. To make it simply add a pinch of *sumak* to the recipe here.

Kookoo now rooz (New Year's omelette) is traditional to the Iranian New Year. It is exactly the same as *kookoo sabzi* with the addition of chopped nuts and dried fruit, and is garnished with thick yoghurt and fennel sprigs.

Serves 4

4oz (110g) spinach
2 bunches spring onions
4 tablespoons chopped parsley
4 tablespoons chopped fresh mint
½ tablespoon dried mint
4 tablespoons snipped chives
2 tablespoons each of three or four more herbs chosen from chervil, watercress, basil, dill, etc

melted smen
6 eggs
¼ teaspoon turmeric
20 strands saffron
aromatic salt and black pepper
½ teaspoon chilli powder (optional)

1 Wash the spinach, flushing out all grit and soil. Dry, de-stalk and shred the leaves into fine strips.

2 Chop the spring onions into thin rings (including the leaves).

3 Mix the spinach, spring onions and herbs together and set aside.

4 Preheat the oven to 325°F/160°C/Gas 3. Select a flan dish about 8–9 inches (20–23cm) in diameter, preferably non-stick, and brush it with melted *smen*.

5 Beat the eggs with a whisk. Add the remaining ingredients and then the greens. Mix well and immediately transfer to the flan dish and cover with aluminium foil.

6 Bake for 20 minutes. Remove the foil and bake for a further 10 minutes, then inspect. The top should be light brown, the inside about cooked. If you want it more solid, cook on for a few minutes longer.

EGGAH MAŞHIYA BAIDH

Egg-stuffed omelette

The egg has been an item of major dietary importance in Egypt since hens were 'battery farmed' in Pharaonic times. Nobody enjoys eggs more than the Egyptians, and no Middle Eastern cookbook would be complete without an Egyptian egg dish. My choice is a fascinating omelette appropriately called an *eggah* in Egypt (and *agga, igga* or *ijja* in other Arabic dialects). This *eggah* has a filling of chopped hard-boiled egg (*baidh*), mixed with fresh herbs and yoghurt. *Tzvazegh* are miniature spiced omelettes.

Serves 4

1 tablespoon smen or olive oil
4 eggs, beaten
½ teaspoon aromatic salt

FILLING
2 tablespoons smen
2 cloves garlic, chopped
¼ teaspoon turmeric

2oz (50g) onions, chopped
4 eggs, hard-boiled and chopped
2 or 3 tablespoons chopped chives,
    mint and parsley
2 tablespoons Greek yoghurt

GARNISH
mustard and cress

1 Make the filling first. Heat the *smen*, and stir-fry the garlic and turmeric for 1 minute. Add the onion and stir-fry for a further 5 minutes. Take off the heat and stir in the chopped eggs, herbs and the yoghurt. Keep warm but not on a direct heat.

2 For the *eggahs*, heat the *smen* in a large flat frying pan. Salt the eggs and pour half into the pan. Cook on medium heat until set, then turn over and cook for a further minute or so, until dried to taste.

3 Turn the *eggah* out on to a plate. Spread half the warm filling on to half the *eggah*. Fold over and keep warm.

4 Repeat stages 2 and 3.

5 To serve, cut each *eggah* in half and garnish with mustard and cress.

CHAPTER 10

THE STAPLES

GRAINS, or the seeds of certain grasses such as barley, corn, maize, millet, oats, rye, wheat and rice, have become essential or 'staple' foods. In areas where drought has always been a common occurrence, the importance of grain throughout history can be measured by frequent written evidence of its suitability for long-term storage. The Bible refers to the years of plenty when the grain stores were filled to bursting, and of famine when supplies were exhausted. The Pharaohs took vessels of grain with them in the pyramids on their passage to the after life.

Wheat in the form of bread has, for millennia, been 'the staff of life' to the peoples of the biblical Mediterranean. Rice, too, is called the 'staff of life' by the Iranians, who also refer to it as 'the soul of Allah'.

WHEAT
About 12,000 years ago, when man began to cultivate the land of the 'fertile crescent', one of the first major crops was wheat. It was eaten in a fairly unrefined form, but a process was developed to make it more palatable. The wheat grain was cracked, partly cooked, dried in the sun and then ground. It was stored until required, when it was reconstituted with water in a porridge-like form. It was probably mankind's first processed food. Today, known as burghul (or *bourgouri*), it is still used in Middle Eastern recipes, particularly the meat stews and salads of Syria and Lebanon.

Wheat grows in many of the countries of the Middle East. Barley, oats and rye are grown in North Africa and Greece, maize in Morocco, Egypt and Turkey.

Couscous
•
Processed semolina grains

Couscous is the ancient staple of the Maghreb, and was undoubtedly the invention of the original inhabitants of the area, the Berbers. Just when can never be known, but it is likely to have been after 2500 BC, when the Berbers became isolated from the Egyptians, and before 1000 BC, by which time wheat had become the bread-making staple in Egypt. We can say this with some certainty because couscous has remained almost exclusively in the Maghreb (reflecting the isolation of the Berbers in the following millennia) and because both bread and the staple that the Arabs brought from India – rice – did not become part of Maghrebi cuisine until around AD 900.

The Berbers may well have been regarded throughout history as primitive hills people, but there is nothing primitive about the preparation of couscous. It requires great skill, and for that reason it is better to use one of the very excellent factory-made brands. Out of interest, couscous is made from wheat. Specifically it is made from semolina, which itself is coarsely ground *durum* (hard) wheat. To make couscous, grains of semolina are spread out, sprinkled with water and rolled with the finger tips with a further sprinkling of fine white flour. The new larger grains are sieved to achieve a constant size (which can vary from small to large). The grains have next to be steamed in a special steamer called a *couscousière*, which is a double boiler with a large water-boiling base and snugly fitting slotted top unit with equally snug-fitting lid. Traditionally these were (and still are) made from pottery, but can also be brass or its modern equivalent, aluminium. When the water is boiling the couscous is placed on muslin in the top unit. The lid is put on and the couscous is steamed for 30 minutes, being aerated by forking it from time to time. It is then removed and spread out in a thin layer on muslin to dry in the hot sun for two days. The dry grains can then be stored indefinitely, and it is in this form that we can buy couscous as a product.

Standard couscous consists of creamy pellets resembling sesame seeds in size and appearance and they must be steamed again, this time with a savoury stew in the bottom which imparts its flavours into the grains. The final dish is served with the strained stew at the centre of a nest of couscous, and the strained gravy separate. The dish (also called couscous) can be meat or fish based, see pages 86, 87 and 113.

This recipe details the steaming of couscous grains.

Serves 4

1lb or 500g packet couscous (see note opposite)

2 tablespoons smen
1 teaspoon aromatic salt

1 I don't have a double-boiler, so I use a largish deep saucepan in which fits very snugly a close-mesh strainer, about 8 inches (20cm) in diameter allowing ample water to boil without the strainer touching it. Boil up the water.

2 Rinse the couscous briefly. Strain well and spread out in a large tray to dry.

3 When the water boils, check that the grains are separate. Line the strainer with a clean tea towel or muslin, and put the strainer on to the saucepan. Use the flaps of the tea towel under the strainer to ensure that no steam escapes. Once steam is flowing through the tea towel, trickle half the couscous on to it and snugly fit the lid. Leave for 3 or 4 minutes, by which time it will be well steamed. Then loosen it with a spoon. Trickle the remaining couscous in and re-fit the lid. Once the steam is flowing through the couscous, turn the heat down to achieve an effective simmer.

4 Every few minutes, aerate the couscous by loosening with a fork. Continue to steam for 20–25 minutes (ensuring that there is ample water).

5 In a separate pan heat up the meat or fish accompaniment (see pages 86, 87 and 113).

6 At the end of stage 4 remove the couscous from the heat. Empty it into the flat tray and add the *smen* and salt, working it in with the fingertips. Pour away any remaining water from the saucepan. Then put the hot stage 5 accompaniment into the couscous saucepan, ensuring there is enough liquid to enable it to simmer for around 20 minutes.

7 Replace the tea towel/muslin in the strainer and put the couscous back in and the strainer over the simmering pan as in stage 3.

8 Simmer for a further 20 minutes, aerating the couscous as in stage 4.

9 To serve, ensure each couscous grain is separate. Make a mound of the couscous in a serving bowl, and a depression in the mound.

10 Strain the accompanying sauce and put the solids into the depression. Serve the sauce in a gravy boat, allowing the diners to add the amount of their choice.

Note: I have seen at least twelve different brands of factory couscous. They come in 1lb or 500g sachets in colourful boxes and all are of perfectly acceptable quality. Most have recipes which state boil the couscous rather than the above steaming. It can be boiled, but this never cooks it to fluffiness in the way that steaming does. In some cases, where the couscous has been pre-cooked, it will require considerably less steaming time than given above. Taste and test it regularly after five minutes, or follow the instructions on the packet.

RICE

Rice originated in China and India, where it has been eaten for at least 9,000 years. The Middle East does not enjoy enough humidity and water to allow for widespread cultivation of rice, but rice has, however, been a fundamental part of its cuisine from when, over 2,500 years ago, it was introduced from India via Iran. It was the Arabs who ensured its spread into North Africa and Spain by the ninth century. Later the Venetians, the Arabs' Mediterranean trading partners, introduced rice to Italy.

Rice grows in small quantities along the northern Nile in Egypt and in the Anatolia area of Turkey. Iran is self-sufficient in rice production, most of it being farmed in the north. Three of the best-quality Iranian extra long-grained rices are *champa*, *berenje sadri* and *dom siyah* (black-tailed). They are superb for cooking and just occasionally they appear in specialist shops in the West. The rice that is widely used in the Middle East is basmati rice, imported from India and Parkistan in huge quantities.

The Iranian dish *pollou* or pillau (from *pollo*, rice), is a combination of basmati rice cooked by absorption with spices and meat or poultry or vegetables. This dish was taken east to India, where *pullao* rice and *pullao* dishes are some of the most important rice dishes of the sub-continent. Westwards, this most famous Persian dish became the basis of *pilav* or *pilaf* in Turkey and Armenia, the *pilafi* dishes of Greece and the paellas of Spain. Steamed plain rice is called *timman* in Iraq, and a similar dish in the Levant area is called *riz mulfalfel*. The North African group of countries – Tunisia, Algeria and Morocco – do not have a rice-eating tradition, preferring couscous (see page 142). Our own word 'rice' is derived from the Arabic *riz* or *roz*, itself from an ancient word *aruz*. The ancient Greek word is *rizi* and the Latin *oryza*. The Hindi word for rice is *chawal*, and the Afghanistan *chaulau* and the Iranian *chelow* are derived from that.

Rice accompanies many Middle Eastern dishes. It is usually enhanced with *smen* (clarified butter) and spices, or it is mixed with other ingredients such as lentils, meat, vegetables or even pasta. Occasionally though, it is nice to have unspiced (plain) rice especially with rich dishes.

There are two basic methods of cooking rice: one consists of boiling it in plenty of water and then draining, and the other of cooking it in a precisely measured amount of water which is completely absorbed by the rice. Both methods give individual and fluffy grains of rice, both can be spiced or unspiced, and both take around the same amount of time to cook. The rice grains swell to a slightly larger size with the boiling method, and they are softer. Using the absorption method, the spicing is cooked in from the early stages of cooking and it is marginally more flavourful.

Basmati rice is a long, narrow-grained, fragrant rice, hard enough to retain a superb *al dente* bite when cooked. All the timings for the recipes which follow are for basmati. Other long-grained or fast-cook rices may require different cooking times and most are unlikely to give the fluffiness and fragrance of basmati.

PLAIN RICE BY BOILING

This is the quickest way to cook rice, and it can be ready to serve in just 15 minutes from the water boiling. Two factors are crucial for this method to work perfectly. Firstly the rice must be basmati rice. Patna or long-grained, quick-cook or other rices will require different timings and will have neither the texture nor the fragrance of basmati. Secondly, it is one of the few recipes in this book which requires *precision timing*. It is essential that for its few minutes on the boil you concentrate on it or else it may over-cook and become stodgy.

A 3oz (75g) portion of dry rice provides an ample helping per person: 2oz (50g) will be a smaller but adequate portion.

Serves 4

8–12oz (225–350g) basmati or
  other long-grained rice
2–3 pints (1·1–1·75 litres) water

1 Pick through the rice to remove grit and particles.

2 Boil the water. It is not necessary to salt it.

3 While it is heating up, rinse the rice briskly with fresh cold water until most of the starch is washed out. Run hot tap water through the rice at the final rinse. This minimizes the temperature reduction of the boiling water when you put the rice into it.

4 When the water is boiling properly, put the rice into the pan. Start timing. Put the lid on the pan until the water comes back to the boil then remove. It takes 8–10 minutes from the start. Stir frequently.

5 After about 6 minutes, taste a few grains. As soon as the centre is no longer brittle, but still has a good *al dente* bite to it, strain off the water. It should seem slightly *under*cooked.

6 Shake off all excess water, then place the strainer on to a dry tea towel which will help remove the last of the water.

7 After a minute place the rice in a pre-warmed serving dish. You can serve it now or put it into a low oven or warming drawer for about half an hour minimum. As it dries, the grains will separate and become fluffy. It can be held in the warmer for several hours if needed.

PLAIN RICE BY ABSORPTION

Cooking rice by a pre-measured ratio of rice to water which is all absorbed into the rice is undoubtedly the best way to do it. Provided that you use basmati rice, the finished grains are longer, thinner and much more fragrant and flavourful than they are after boiling.

The method is easy, but many cookbooks make it sound far too complicated. Instructions invariably state that you must use a tightly lidded pot and precise water quantity and heat levels, and never lift the lid during the boiling process, etc, etc. However, I lift the lid, I might stir the rice, and I've even cooked rice by absorption without a lid. Also, if I've erred on the side of too little water, I've added a bit during 'the boil'. (Too much water is an unresolvable problem.) It's all naughty, rule-breaking stuff, but it still seems to work.

Another factor, always omitted in other people's books, is the time factor. They all say or imply that rice must be served as soon as 'the boil' is completed. This causes stress to the cook who believes that there is no margin of error in time and method. In reality, the longer you give the rice to dry, the fluffier and more fragrant it will be. So it can be cooked well in advance of being required for serving. For after the initial 'boil' and 10-minute simmer the rice is quite sticky, and it needs to 'relax'. After 30 minutes it can be served and is fluffy, but it can be kept in a warm place for much longer – improving in fluffiness all the time.

Cooking rice by this method does need practice. You may need one or two goes at it. Here are some tips for the newcomer:

1 Choose a pan, preferably with a lid, that can be used both on the stove and in the oven. Until you have had lots of practice, always use the same pan, so that you become familiar with it.

2 Keep a good eye on the clock. The timing of 'the boil' is important or you'll burn the bottom of the rice.

3 Use basmati rice.

4 If you intend to let the rice cool down for serving later, or the next day, or to freeze it, do not put it in the warmer. It is better slightly under-cooked for these purposes.

Note: 10oz (300g) is 2 teacups of dry rice, and 20fl oz (1 pint/570ml) is about $1\frac{1}{3}$ volume of water to 1 of rice. This 10:20 (2 teacups : 1 pint) combination is easy to remember, but do step up or step down the quantities as required in proportion. For small appetites, for instance, use 8oz (225g) rice : 16fl oz (450ml) water. For large appetites use 12oz (350g) rice : 24fl oz (685ml) water.

Serves 4

10oz (300g) basmati rice
20fl oz (1 pint/570ml) water

1 Soak the rice in extra water to cover for about half an hour.

2 Rinse it until the rinse water runs more or less clear, then strain.

3 Bring the measured water to the boil in a saucepan (as heavy as possible, and with a lid), or a casserole dish at least twice the volume of the strained rice.

4 As soon as it is boiling add the rice and stir in well.

5 As soon as it starts bubbling put the lid on the pan and reduce the heat to under half and leave well alone for 8 minutes.

6 Inspect. Has the liquid absorbed on top? If not, replace the lid and leave for 2 more minutes. If and when it has, stir the rice well, ensuring it is not sticking to the bottom. Now taste. It should not be brittle in the middle. If it is, add a little more water and heat for a little longer.

7 Place the saucepan or casserole in an oven preheated to its very lowest setting. You can serve the rice at once, but the longer you leave it, the more separate the grains will be. An hour is fine, but it will be quite safe and happy left for several hours.

TIMMAN

Fried rice Iraqi style

This dish is called *riz m'falfal,* in the Lebanon, *beyaz pilav* (white rice) in Turkey and *dami* in Iran.

Serves 4

rice (see method)
2 tablespoons smen
½ teaspoon aromatic salt

METHOD 1, BY BOILING

1 Follow the recipe for 'plain rice by boiling' on page 145 through to the end of stage 6.

2 Wash and dry the saucepan and heat the *smen* in it. Put the rice and salt in and stir-fry for a couple of minutes, until it is warm. Proceed to the end of stage 7 of the plain rice method.

METHOD 2, BY ABSORPTION

Serves 4

1 Follow the recipe for plain rice by absorption on page 147 to the end of stage 2.

2 In a separate pan boil up the water.

3 In a saucepan (as heavy as possible and with a lid), or a casserole dish at least twice the volume of the strained rice, heat the *smen*.

4 Add the rice and the salt and stir-fry it, ensuring the oil coats the rice and that it heats up (about 2 minutes). Add the boiled water and stir it well into the rice.

5 Follow stages 5–7 of plain rice by absorption.

CHELLOW

Crusty Iranian rice

They were eating this dish in Persia 3,000 years ago and it is still regarded as Iran's most important rice dish. It must be cooked by absorption, not only to achieve the best flavours, but to create a crust on the bottom of the cooking pot. Called *tahdig* in Iranian or *hakkakah* in Arabic, the crust is regarded as the best part of the rice, rather like the crusty end of fresh bread is to us, and it is always offered to guests. I use a little more rice for this recipe to allow for some wastage in making the crust.

Serves 4

12–16oz (350–450g) basmati rice
1 tablespoon smen
½ teaspoon aromatic salt
20 strands saffron (optional)

1 Follow the *timman* rice by absorption method (previous recipe), through to the end of stage 6 of the method on page 147. Do not stir the rice at any stage, otherwise the crust can't form at the bottom of the pan. At the end of stage 6, apply full heat to the pan for 2–3 minutes, then go to stage 7.

2 To serve, remove the fluffy rice first, carefully teasing it off the crust. Then scrape the crust from the pan bottom. Not everyone likes this Iranian delicacy, so offer it on a separate plate.

TAHDIG or HAKKAKAH

Rice crust

A variation on *chellow* is to grate peeled raw potato and fry it in the saucepan at the end of stage 3 of the *timman* recipe referred to. Add the rice, but don't stir it into the potatoes, then the boiled water and proceed with stage 5.

POLLOU

Iranian rice

Pollous are another delightful Iranian speciality. The rice is cooked with a choice of fragrant spices and *smen*. *Pollous* often include meat or fish or vegetables in the cooking, but here the recipe calls just for aromatic spices. It can be cooked by the boiling method (see page 145), fried spices being added at the end, or by the absorption method (see page 147), frying the spices early on.

Serves 4

8–12oz (225–350g) basmati rice
2–3 pints (1·2–1·75 litres) water
  (boiling method)
4 tablespoons smen
20 strands saffron

SPICES (ALL WHOLE)
4 green cardamoms
4 cloves
$\frac{1}{2}$ teaspoon white cummin seeds
$\frac{1}{4}$ teaspoon black cummin seeds
$\frac{1}{4}$ teaspoon fennel seeds
2 inch (5 cm) piece cassia bark

METHOD 1, BY BOILING

1 Follow the recipe for 'plain rice by boiling' on page 145 through to the end of stage 6.

2 Rinse and dry the saucepan or casserole dish, and heat the *smen*. Stir-fry the spices for no more than 30 seconds. Add the rice and stir-fry until it is warm (about 2 minutes). Proceed to stage 7 of the recipe for 'plain rice by boiling', adding the saffron at this point.

METHOD 2, BY ABSORPTION

Serves 4

1 Follow the recipe for 'plain rice by absorption' on page 147 to the end of stage 2.

2 In a separate pan, boil up the water.

3 In a saucepan (as heavy as possible and with a lid), or a casserole dish at least twice the volume of the strained rice, heat the *smen*. Stir-fry the spices for no more than 30 seconds.

4 Add the rice and stir-fry it, ensuring the oil coats the rice, for enough time to warm it up (about 2 minutes). Add the boiling water and stir it well into the rice.

5 Follow stages 5–7 of the method for 'plain pice by absorption', adding the saffron at the end of stage 6.

ROZ BI SHA'RIYAH

Rice with vermicelli

The combination of grain with pasta may seem unlikely, but it is, however, one of the most popular dishes in the Mediterranean Middle East. As far as I can tell this dish goes back to the Middle Ages, devised at a time when Arab links with Venice were at their height. Rice was traded to Italy, pasta returned to the East. One mixed marriage was this Jordanian recipe.

Serves 4

6–8oz (175–225g) basmati rice
2–4oz (50–110g) vermicelli
3 tablespoons smen
3 tablespoons pine nuts, roasted

1 Follow the recipe for 'plain rice by absorption' on page 147, to the end of stage 2.

2 Break the vermicelli sticks into 1 inch (2·5cm) pieces.

3 In a separate pan, boil up the water.

4 In a saucepan (as heavy as possible, with a lid) or a casserole dish at least twice the volume of the rice and vermicelli, heat the *smen*.

5 Add the rice and the vermicelli and stir-fry until coated with the oil and they are warmed (about 2 minutes). Add the boiled water and stir-fry it well in.

6 Follow stages 5–7 of 'plain rice by absorption'. Garnish with the pine nuts.

RIZ EL TAMMAR

Rice with dates

Libya's principal culinary asset is the date – in fact dozens of species of date – and Libya consumes more rice than its Maghrebi neighbours. The two together make for a dish of great character, to accompany savoury dishes.

Serves 4

8–12oz (225–350g) basmati rice
2oz (50g) dates, stoned and
    chopped
2 teaspoons orange-blossom water

$\frac{1}{2}$ teaspoon aromatic salt
2 tablespoons smen
1 tablespoon pistachio nuts

1 Cook the rice either by the boiling method on page 145 or by absorption, page 147.

2 In either case add the remaining ingredients and mix them in well after the cooking stage and prior to the rice 'resting' in the warmer.

BREAD

The ancient Egyptians mastered the art of fermentation to make wine and beer some 4,000 years ago. They also discovered how to ferment dough (leavening), and developed the baking of bread. By 1500 BC round flat loaves, called *aiysh*, were sold at their bakeries. *Aiysh* in Egyptian means 'life', and bread has long been called 'the staff (support) of life'. The importance of bread remains undiminished, with the method of baking *aiysh* unchanged to this day, and similar bread is to be found all round the Middle East. Shapes and sizes vary a little from discs of around 6 inches (15cm) to ovals of 8–10 inches (20–25cm), but the basic dough is the same. This type of bread is called *khoubiz* or *khubz* in Arabia and the Levant; *kmaj* in Lebanon (with pocket) or *mafroudha* (without); *saluf* in Yemen; *shrak* in Jordan and Palestine, and *aiysh shami* in Syria. In Israel it is called *matzo*, whilst in Greece it is *taftoon*. A larger oval Iranian variant is called *nane lavash*, which is the derivative of the celebrated *naan* bread of India. Equally well known is the pitta of Greece and Turkey. In Morocco the standard bread is *khobz* made from unleavened plain white flour and rolled into round flat discs about 12 inches (30cm) in diameter and 2 inches (5cm) high. Unique to Morocco is *hasha* or *matlou*, a leavened bread made from semolina, and *ksra*, also leavened and made from semolina but mixed with flour and spiced with sesame and aniseed.

There are many other types of bread to be found in the Middle East, such as the Iranian *barbari*. Made from white flour, it is 2 inches (5cm) long and 4 inches (10cm) wide after baking with four ribs. The *sangyak*, also from Iran, is 2 feet 6 inches wide (about 75cm), oiled on top and baked on hot pebbles until it bubbles. The Yemen produces two breads of distinction – *maluj* from a barley dough, and *bint-al-sahn*, where sheets of thinly rolled yeasty dough are spread with *samneh* (see page 36), placed in layers one on top of the other, then baked. Israel's bagels and *pretzels* are especially well known in bakeries of modern Israel, as well as those of Jewish communities all over the world. *Samouli* is a type of Arabian French loaf stick, varying in size from very short to quite long. A variation of the bagel appears as *samit* in Egypt, *kaak* in the Levant, and *simit* in Turkey. It is a sesame seed-sprinkled, golden-baked ring popular at breakfast with yoghurt and honey. *Korek* or *charek* is a tea-time sweet bun containing raisins, sugar, milk and oil in the dough. It originated in Turkey but can be found all over the region. Many breads are made with a stuffing or topping. Olives are mixed into the dough of the *zeytin* in Turkey, where they also make a cake-like bread from cornflour and yoghurt. Onions, herbs, chillies and cheese can also be used as a spicy topping, spread on before baking – for example, the Yemeni *hilbeh* with fenugreek and coriander paste (see page 50).

Dough making

Basically, once you have mastered this simple dough recipe you can make all the breads in this chapter. The secrets of success lie in the first kneading, which must achieve a thorough blending of the ingredients, and a good proving (rising) time in a warm place. The dough should be elastic without being sticky, and it should feel satisfying to handle in that it is pliable, springy and soft.

DOUGH MIX

1lb (450g) strong white flour (huwmara) OR *1lb (450g) brown chapatti flour (khashkar)* OR *wholemeal flour*

1oz (25g) fresh yeast tepid water

1 Dissolve the fresh yeast in a little warm water.

2 Put the flour in a *warmed* bowl, make a well in the centre, and pour in the dissolved yeast (or 2 tablespoons plain yoghurt can be used in the absence of yeast).

3 Gently mix into the flour, and add enough tepid water to make a firm dough.

4 Remove from the bowl and knead on a floured board until well combined. Return the dough to the bowl and leave in a warm place, covered, for a couple of hours to rise. Your dough, when risen, should double in size. It should be bubbly, stringy and like elastic.

5 'Knock back' the dough by kneading it down to its original size. Add the recipe spices.

6 Proceed to the recipe of your choice between this page and page 158.

KHOUBIZ or KHOBZ

Arab bread

Khoubiz is the standard, flat, slightly levened bread to be found all over the Levant and the Gulf, and as far afield as Morocco (where it is called *khobz*) and the other Maghreb countries. In Jordan and Palestine the identical bread is called *sh'raak*. Basically *khoubiz* is a round, flat disc varying in size from country to country between 6 inches (15cm) and 12 inches (30cm) in diameter. *Khoubiz* has been made for thousands of years, and the only change is the recent option of using white flour (*huwmara*). Finely ground wholemeal flour (*khashkar*), using a hard wheat grain, is the traditional norm. Western wholemeal flour suffices, but, if you can get it, use chapatti flour.

Makes 4

1 quantity of white or brown dough (see opposite)

1 Follow all the dough-making recipe stages.

2 Divide the dough into four pieces and make into balls. Roll each into a disc about 9 inches (23cm) in diameter. Let stand to prove while oven heats up to 400°F/200°C/Gas 6.

3 Put the discs on floured oven trays. Prick them with a fork to prevent them rising, then bake for 8–10 minutes. Serve hot.

MAN'AIYSH or MN'AQISH

Lebanese spicy bread

Here the standard *khoubiz* bread is rolled into discs about 5 inches (13cm) in diameter by $\frac{1}{4}$ inch (6mm) thick. The disc is made slightly concave, then liberally brushed with a mixture of olive oil and *za'atar* before being baked. Prick the discs to prevent them puffing up.

KHOUBIZ BASALI

Syrian onion bread

Identical to the above, but the topping is finely chopped raw onion mixed with a little ground cummin and coriander and dried mint.

SALUF BI HILBEH

Yemeni spicy bread

Yemeni people adore spices almost as much as Indians. In this case spread the disc with *hilbeh* (see page 50), then bake as usual.

PITTA BREAD

Greek/Turkish oval bread

Probably the most celebrated bread from the Middle East is the pitta, that delicious, oval-shaped, flat bread with the pocket, so convenient for holding food. Pitta is, in fact, simply a variant of *khoubiz*, the main difference being in its shape. Indeed in Syria it is called *khubz shami* or *aiysh shami*, whilst in the Gulf it is called *khubz arabi*. The traditional pitta shape is an oval about 8 × 6 inches (20 × 15cm) and $\frac{3}{16}$ inch (2–3mm) thick. It must always have a pocket, called *mutbag*.

Pittas are easy enough to make, and the way to achieve the pocket is to knead the dough well, leaving it to rise and expand in a warm place, and then bake in a hottish oven. If the pocket is not required, prick the rolled-out bread with a fork. An Armenian variation of pitta is *pideh*: it uses wholemeal flour, and white sesame seeds are pressed on to the dough before baking.

1 quantity of dough (see page 152)

1 Follow the dough-making recipe on page 152–3 to stage 6.

2 Divide the dough into six pieces and then roll into oval shapes as described above. Let stand to prove whilst the oven heats up to 400°F/200°C/Gas 6.

3 Put the discs on floured oven trays. Bake for 8–10 minutes. Serve hot.

AIYSH

Egyptian bread

Follow the previous recipe exactly, using a brown dough. Shape into four discs of about 6–8 inches (15–20cm) in diameter and $\frac{3}{8}$ inch (9mm) thick. When cooked the *aiysh* puffs up like a balloon and it should be quite soft, which is ideal for scooping up food.

BARBARI

Iranian white bread

Barbari is rectangular in shape and can vary in size from 2×4 inches (5×10cm) to 6×12 inches (15×30cm). It traditionally has four ribs or grooves, scored with a knife. I prefer to make this to the small size as they look so attractive. They are usually unspiced, but optional varieties include dabbing them in either sesame, cummin or caraway seeds before baking.

Makes 8

1 quantity white dough (see page 152)

1 Follow the dough-making recipe on page 152–3 to stage 6.

2 Divide the dough into eight to twelve pieces. Shape them into small rectangles, then roll them out to 2×4 inches (5×10cm) $\times \frac{1}{2}$ inch (1cm) thick. Score them on the top almost completely through four times with a sharp knife. Put them on floured oven trays allowing room between each for expansion during proving. Let them stand to prove whilst the oven heats up to 400°F/200°C/Gas 6.

3 Then bake for 8–10 minutes. Serve hot.

RAGAYIG

Arabian crisp bread

The recipe for this completely unleavened bread most certainly pre-dates *aiysh*, *khoubiz* and pitta, and probably originated when man first learned to cultivate wheat over 9,000 years ago. The dough is very simple, being a wholemeal or plain white flour and water. It is kneaded and rolled into thin discs, which are slowly baked at the local bakers (*furunji*) for a few pennies, or they are cooked over charcoal on a *sorj* (an inverted cast-iron, wok-like implement). When cooked the discs are eaten at once or they are further dried in the sun to crisp them off. After this treatment they can be stored in a lidded earthenware pot for months. An Iranian variant is called *lavash* and in Turkey it is *kavgir*.

Makes 8

1 quantity of brown or white
dough, yeast omitted (see page 152)

1 Mix the flour and enough warm water in a bowl to make a firm dough.

2 Remove from the bowl and knead on a floured board until well combined. Return to the bowl and leave the dough for half an hour or so. It won't rise, but it will have a better elasticity.

3 Divide the dough into eight pieces and roll out into discs around 9 inches (23cm) diameter by $\frac{1}{8}$ inch (3mm) thick. Place the disc on floured oven trays and bake in the oven at 400°F/200°C/Gas 6 for 10–12 minutes. When cool, they can be broken into pieces and stored like biscuits in an airtight tin. If they lose crispness re-bake for a few minutes.

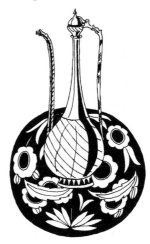

PAKTAKATA

Lebanese sweet Lenten bread

This delightful 'surprise' bread is traditionally made only during Lent by the small Christian community in the Levant. The dough contains syrup or honey and is rolled out into a thick disc about 6 inches (15cm) in diameter and $\frac{1}{2}$ inch (1cm) thick. The surface of the disc is often highly decorated with squirls and squiggles made by running the tip of a knife or fork over it. Buried inside the dough is a clean silver coin (it's rather like our Christmas pudding tradition), and the children vie with each other to get the coins – and that's the surprise.

Makes 4

1 quantity of white dough (see
  page 152)
$1\frac{1}{2}$–2 tablespoons honey
4 clean 'silver' coins

1 Follow the dough-making recipe on page 152–3, adding the honey and making the dough to the end of stage 6.

2 Divide the dough into four pieces and make into balls. Place one coin into the centre of each ball, then roll each out to discs as stated above. Decorate them as you wish. Place them on floured oven trays.

3 Bake for 10–12 minutes in the oven preheated to 400°F/200°C/Gas 6. Serve hot.

BAGELS

Jewish crusty bread rings

Bagels have been popularized by Jewish communities the world over. They are golden brown, hard crusty rings, said to have been created by a Polish Jew in the Middle Ages to celebrate the winning of a major war. Be that as it may, they are now as popular in Israel as they are elsewhere. The unusual feature of bagel cooking is that the rings are blanched in boiling water (which removes starch and makes the bagel lighter) before they are baked. Bagels can be baked with a variety of toppings including chopped onion, sesame seeds, blue poppy seeds, raisins and honey, and they can be eaten at any time.

My favourite time is in the small hours of the morning. Why then?

Because you can get hot, freshly baked bagels 24 hours a day in London's East End at 'The Bagel House', 100 Brick Lane, E1. As there are so few all-night watering-holes in the great city, this is a life-saver for insomniacs. Ask any taxi driver to take you there – that's where they all go anyway.

Makes 16

1 quantity of white dough (see
page 152)
1 egg
2 teaspoons sugar
2 tablespoons smen or butter
½ teaspoon salt

TO GLAZE
1 egg, beaten
sesame seeds

1 Follow the dough-making recipe on page 152, adding the egg, sugar, *smen* and salt, to the end of stage 6.

2 Divide the dough into four pieces and sub-divide each piece into a further four pieces to create sixteen equal-sized pieces of dough.

3 Roll one piece of dough into a cable of about 8 inches (20cm) in length and ½ inch (1cm) thickness. Curl into a ring, ensuring that the join is very secure. Repeat with the other fifteen cables. Leave the rings to prove in a warm place for around 15 minutes.

4 Meanwhile, preheat the oven to 400°F/200°C/Gas 6, and bring a pan of water to the boil.

5 Then immerse one ring in the boiling water. When it rises to the surface (a minute or so), remove it and put it on a floured or greased oven tray. Repeat with the other rings.

6 Glaze each ring with the beaten egg and sprinkle on sesame seeds.

7 Bake for 15 minutes, by which time they should be a nice golden colour.

KA'AK

Variations of the bagel are found in many Middle Eastern countries. In Tunisia and Libya they are called *ka'kis* or *ka'kis bil semsem*; in the Levant *ka'ak*; in Armenia *choerig*; and in Egypt *semit*. In other countries *semit* are still ring shaped, but thicker than *ka'ak*. In Turkey *semit* street-sellers carry the rings around on long poles. In Armenia the *choerig* has evolved from a ring into a snail shape. In all other respects it is the same as *semit*.

To make *ka'ak* or *choerig* follow the bagel recipe. Add 1 teaspoon *mahlab* to the dough mix (see page 181).

CHAPTER · 11

DESSERTS AND SWEET THINGS

TO SAY the people of the Middle East have a sweet tooth is an understatement. Probably the most celebrated Middle Eastern sweet pastries are baklava and *kadayif*, which are made from the thinnest filo pastry – baklava in layers, *kadayif* in shredded form – and drenched in sticky syrup. My selection of sweet recipes includes both of these, as well as a selection of puddings including *m'hancha* (the intriguing Moroccan pastry 'snake cake', so called because it is curled like a sleeping serpent) and *irmik helvasi* from Turkey (fried semolina pudding called *sujee helva* in the Levant). Pancakes are represented by two ultra-tasty recipes – *blintze* from Israel, and *ataif* from Bahrain.

A dessert with a delightful name – *um m'ali* (Ali's mum's pud) – is in fact a rather excellent bread and butter pudding. And no Middle Eastern sweet chapter would be complete without a recipe using the prolific date.

If none of these take your fancy you may want to provide something simpler. Fresh fruit (*fawakah*) is an obvious and always welcome choice. Indigenous to the Middle East, and amongst the earliest fruit to be cultivated was the apple (*toofa*). The grape (*einab*), pomegranate (*ruman*), fig (*tiin*), date (*tamar*), cherry (*karaz*), and pear (*tmar*), are equally ancient. Apricots (*meeshmeesh*) and peaches (*kukh*) originated in China, and had reached the Middle East centuries before Christ. Oranges (*burtukul*), also from China, came later. From India in the early trading days came guavas (*guafa*), bananas (*mohz*), mangos (*manga*), limes (*limoon*) and melons (*bateeq*). The only major fruit to have been introduced to the Arab world from America was the strawberry (*farawleh*).

Ice cream is very popular all over the Middle East and can be made with water (sorbet style), with milk, and with thick rich cream, so it is quite legitimate to serve with any Middle Eastern menu, if for no other reason than its Arabic name – *booza-booza*!

159

BAKLAVA

Sweet crisp pastries

Baklava is undoubtedly one of the most celebrated and best-known sweet pastries from the Middle East. It is readily available in Greek, Turkish and Middle Eastern restaurants and delicatessens all over the world. Each baklava is a diamond-shaped assembly of layered pastry, punctuated with dots of chopped nuts and butter, then cooked to a gorgeous golden colour. It is laced with a sticky syrup and is served cold. Needless to say, it is high in calories, sticky and dripping, and is quite irresistible. The ancient Greeks had a dish along these lines, but it is certain that once again, as with *boreks*, it was the chefs of the Ottomans who developed it into the superb sweetmeat it is today. It is found all over the Middle East with occasional variations in spelling (eg, *baglavah, b'learwa*).

Delicious though it is, the commercial version is sometimes rather soggy because it has sat marinating in its syrup for two or three days. It can also be too sweet. The home-made version is easy enough to make provided you don't let the filo pastry dry out. Even made the day before, it will be much crisper than its commercial counterpart.

Enough for 12–18 servings

1lb 2oz (500g) packet of filo pastry
approx. 2oz (50g) smen or clarified
   butter

SYRUP
$\frac{1}{2}$ pint (300ml) water
8oz (225g) granulated white sugar
2 tablespoons Greek honey
   (optional)

1 tablespoon lemon juice
1 teaspoon rose water or orange-
   blossom water

FILLING
8–10oz (225–300g) pistachios,
   walnuts, hazelnuts or almonds,
   finely chopped, mixed with 2
   teaspoons powdered cinnamon

1 Make the syrup first, so that it is chilled ready for stage 9. Boil the water. Add the sugar (and honey), stir until it dissolves, then stir occasionally for the next 10 minutes as it thickens.

2 When at pouring consistency, take off the heat. Add the lemon juice and rose water or orange-blossom water. Stir in, then cool the syrup in the fridge for at least 2 hours. If it thickens too much as it chills, add cold water to thin it.

RIGHT, CLOCKWISE FROM THE TOP: *Baklava* (sweet crisp pastries) above, *El M'Hancha* (almond snake cake) page 163, *Kadayif* (sweet, crisp, shredded pastries) page 162, *Ataif* (syrupy pancakes) page 167, *Irmik Helvasi* (fried semolina pudding) page 165.

3 Preheat the oven to 350°F/180°C/Gas 4, and melt the *smen* or clarified butter in a small pan. Choose an oven tray about 12 × 10 inches (30 × 25cm) with sides at least 2 inches (5cm) high. Brush it with *smen*.

4 Have a damp clean tea towel to hand. Open the filo packet. Cut the entire bunch of sheets to the size of the oven tray. Cover the sheets with the tea towel to stop the filo drying out (which it does fast). *Note:* If the packet size is the standard 12 × 20 inches (30 × 50cm) halve it to 12 × 10 inches (30 × 25cm) and repack the spare half in a plastic bag for future use.

5 Take one sheet of filo (cover the rest), and put it into the oven tray. Brush it with *smen*. Repeat with the next five sheets. Do not press the sheets together. Drop them lightly on top of each other. This results in lighter puff pastry. Sprinkle with a good coating of spiced nuts.

6 Repeat stage 5 three more times, using all the sheets in the packet (usually 24).

7 Traditionally baklava is cut into diamond shapes (see below). This is partly done now and is finished after cooking. Cut from the top sheet but not right through to the bottom; go about two-thirds down.

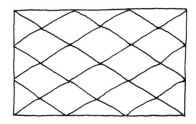

8 Bake for 30 minutes, then inspect. It should now be pale gold. Up the heat to 425°F/220°C/Gas 7, and bake for 10–15 minutes more. Inspect during this time. Remove when it is golden in colour.

9 Keep the baklava on the oven tray and immediately finish the cutting into individual pieces. Without delay pour the cold syrup on to the piping hot pastry. This achieves maximum penetration of the syrup.

10 Cool in the fridge (for at least 3 hours), after which it can be served. Baklavas will keep in the fridge for 3–4 days.

LEFT, CLOCKWISE FROM THE TOP: *Lose Hiloo* (sugared almonds) page 170, *Sephardi Tamar* (stuffed dates) page 168, *Q'Ahwah Arabiya* (Arab coffee) page 173, *Rahat Lokum* (Turkish Delight) page 169, *Chai Bi Na'na* (Moroccan mint tea) page 175.

KADAYIF or KUNAFAH

Sweet, crisp, shredded pastries

Kadayif is a variation of the previous baklava recipe, and is equally well known. Indeed some people prefer it to baklava. (It is pronounced *kat-aiee-eef* in Turkey, called *kataifi* in Greece, and *kunafah, konafeh, k'nafi,* etc, in Arab lands.) The dough is a finely shredded filo, its strands as thin as vermicelli. It vaguely resembles shredded wheat in appearance but not in taste or colour.

Several variations of this delicious pastry exist – *kunafah bil eishta* is topped with thick Arab clotted cream, *kunafah bil jibn* is topped with *peynir* cheese, balurieh is the Syrian version and is slowly baked at a low oven temperature so that it is a creamy white rather than a deep golden colour.

If filo is hard to make at home, *kadayif* dough is nigh on impossible. Filo dough is watered down to batter consistency. It is then poured swiftly through a special sieve in spirals on to a huge hot griddle pan. The large white lattice is deftly scooped up and gently folded whilst soft. It is in this form that it can be bought in 1lb 2oz (500g) packs from delicatessens.

Serves 4

1lb 2oz (500g) packet kadayif dough	*syrup, as for baklava (see page 160)*
approx. 2oz (50g) smen or clarified butter	*filling, as for baklava (see page 160)*

1 Pre-heat the oven, melt the *smen* and grease an oven tray as for baklava (see page 160).

2 Open the *kadayif* packet. Tease out the strands of dough, and halve it. Put the first half in the oven tray, covering the second half with a tea towel. Without pressing it down, fit it into the tray. Brush melted butter into as many of the strands as possible, working it in with your fingers. Then pour on the nuts.

3 Put the remaining half of the pastry on top, again buttering as many strands as possible. Gently shape it on to the oven tray.

4 Bake in the oven as stage 8 of the baklava recipe.

5 Remove from the oven and immediately pour the syrup over the hot pastry.

6 Serve hot or cold, cutting into individual portions as required.

EL M'HANCHA

Almond snake cake

The Moroccan snake cake appears at the drop of a hat at any special occasions (or, any occasion for that matter). *Warkah* pastry (or filo) is used and it is stuffed with almond paste rolled into a very long pencil, then coiled round and round into a snake-like (*hancha*) spiral. After baking, it is dusted with icing sugar, criss-crossed with lines of ground cinnamon. It looks good and, believe me, it is good. It is quite easy to make too.

Serves 4 (or more)

6 sheets filo pastry, 20 × 12 inches
  (50 × 30cm)
flour and water paste
1 egg, beaten

FILLING
8oz (225g) ground almonds
1 tablespoon icing sugar

1 teaspoon powdered cinnamon
3fl oz (75ml) orange-blossom
  water
2 tablespoons smen or butter,
  melted

TO GARNISH
icing sugar
powdered cinnamon

1 Make the filling first. Mix together the almonds, sugar and cinnamon, and add the orange-blossom water and melted *smen*. Mix into a paste of thick, mouldable texture – not wet – but you'll need to add a little water to achieve it. Roll into six pencil shapes slightly shorter than the length of the filo sheets.

2 Preheat the oven to 375°F/190°C/Gas 5, and have two clean, damp tea towels ready.

3 Open the filo packet, take out six sheets and cover five with one towel. Spread the sixth sheet flat on a large work surface, and place the first almond pencil on to it. Roll the sheet up as tightly as you can, and cover with the second towel.

4 Spread the next sheet of filo out and place the next almond pencil on to it. Run a smear of flour and water paste down one short edge. Overlap the first rolled-up pastry on to this pasted edge, then roll *it* up to make a double-length pencil. Now curl this double pencil into a tight spiral. Place on a greased round flan tin.

5 Repeat with the next two sheets and add them on to the spiral in the flan tin (overlap the join so it won't show).

6 Repeat with the last two sheets and your spiral should now be 10–12 inches (25–30cm) in diameter.

7 Glaze the coil with the beaten egg.

8 Put the flan tray into the oven and bake for 10 minutes. It will now be pale golden in colour. Remove and turn the spiral over. Bake for a further 10 minutes or so or until it is the colour gold of your choice (pale to dark).

9 Remove again. Turn the spiral back over again, and sprinkle with icing sugar. Put it on a serving plate and carefully draw a grid of brown lines of cinnamon powder over the white sugar.

RIGHAIF

Curly pastry ribbons

If you are fortunate enough to visit a Moroccan pastry shop, you had better not be on a diet, because it will be stacked full of juicy, syrupy, crisp golden delights and temptation. *Righaif* are bound to be there, squirly curly ribbons of pastry wound around into a circle about 3 inches (7·5cm) in diameter. They are deep-fried to a golden brown, then laced with honey and sprinkled with sesame.

A version is called *shebhakiah* using the same pastry but shaped into small flower-petal shapes.

Makes 12 righaifs

8oz (225g) plain white flour
½oz (15g) fresh yeast
2 teaspoons granulated white
   sugar
1 egg
3 tablespoons smen or butter,
   melted

½ teaspoon salt
oil for deep frying
8oz (225g) honey
1 tablespoon sesame seeds

1 To make the pastry, sieve the flour into a large mixing bowl.

2 Dissolve the yeast in about 100ml (4fl oz) warm water, then add the sugar.

3 Mix this into the flour with the egg, *smen* and salt and sufficient water to make a stiffish dough.

4 Knead it well, then leave it to rest for a while. Heat the deep-frying oil to 375°F/190°C (chip-frying temperature), and heat the honey gently in a separate pan.

5 Divide the dough into four pieces and shape each into a square.

6 Roll the first square out to a large thin shape, then using a curly pastry wheel, cut to a square with about 10 inch (25cm) sides. Cut the square into six strips.

7 Pick up two strips, join them together and curl them into an irregular circle. Immediately immerse this in the deep-frying oil and fry until golden (about 6–8 minutes).

8 Drain, then immerse in the hot simmering honey for 10 seconds. Remove and sprinkle with sesame seeds.

9 As soon as the first one is frying, repeat stage 7 until there are three *righaifs* cooking together. Remove them in the order they went in.

10 Repeat stages 6, 7, 8 and 9 until all twelve are cooked. They are normally served cold.

IRMIK HELVASI

Fried semolina pudding

This Turkish pudding is much more delicious than its simple name suggests. It is quick to make, although a certain amount of stirring is required. In essence it is a stir-fry of the ingredients, cooked to a lovely pale brown colour and with a soft paste-like texture. It can be served cold, but it is infinitely nicer hot. As a study of the ingredients shows it is extremely rich, so small helpings are in order. Variations of this pudding are found all over the Middle East – and in India. In the Levant it is called *sujee helva*.

Serves 4

4oz (110g) butter	*$\frac{1}{4}$ pint (150ml) double cream*
2oz (50g) pine nuts	*5oz (150g) brown sugar*
9oz (250g) semolina	*3 or 4 drops vanilla essence*
$\frac{1}{2}$ pint (300ml) milk	

1 Melt the butter on a medium heat. Add the pine nuts and stir-fry for 2 minutes.

2 Add the semolina and stir-fry until it becomes golden (about 5 minutes).

3 Add the milk, cream and sugar bit by bit in about four or five batches, stirring it until it thickens each time. Serve hot or, if preferred, place it on a flat oven tray and cool. Cut into slices when cold.

BLINTZE

Sweet cheese pancakes

These absolutely delicious Israeli cream cheese-filled pancakes are either served as a savoury dish (with salt), or sweet, as in this recipe from the stunning Seven Arches restaurant in Jerusalem's Hotel Inter-Continental.

Makes 12–14 pancakes

PANCAKES
4oz (110g) plain white flour
2oz (50g) butter, melted, plus extra
  for frying
2 eggs, beaten
½ pint (300ml) milk, warmed
1 tablespoon sugar
3 or 4 drops vanilla essence

FILLING
8oz (225g) curd cheese or labnah
  (see page 39)
¼ pint (150ml) thick soured cream
2 tablespoons brown sugar
1 teaspoon powdered cinnamon
1 teaspoon ground green
  cardamom

GARNISH
icing sugar
lemon wedges

1 To make the pancakes, sift the flour into a bowl and mix in the butter, eggs, warm milk, sugar and vanilla. Mix well and leave to stand for about 10 minutes. The batter should be of pouring consistency.

2 Mix the filling ingredients together.

3 In a very hot omelette or griddle pan, heat a little butter. Pour in enough batter which, when 'swirled' around the pan, makes a thin pancake.

4 Cook to set, then turn over and briefly cook the other side. Turn it out and place some of the filling across the centre of the pancake.

5 Tuck in two sides then roll it up to create a cylinder, and keep warm. Serve with a dusting of icing sugar and a squeeze of lemon.

ATAIF or QATAAYIF

Syrupy pancakes

All over the Arab Islamic world these pancakes make a symbolic and eagerly awaited appearance to mark the end of the month-long annual fast of Ramadan (bearing a slight comparison with our pancakes on Shrove Tuesday tradition). They are served hot or cold, folded to a semicircle or rolled up, then drenched with hot syrup or honey and served with or without the thick Arab clotted cream (*kaymak*) and/or chopped nuts. There is also a savoury version using a cream cheese filling mixed with herbs. This recipe is from Bahrain.

Makes 12–14 pancakes

THE PANCAKES
as for blintze (see opposite).

FILLING
*8oz (225g) chopped walnuts or
   other nuts*
2 tablespoons brown sugar
*1 teaspoon ground green
   cardamom*
½ teaspoon grated nutmeg

SYRUP ('ATARI)
¼ pint (150ml) golden syrup
2fl oz (50ml) honey
2 tablespoons lemon juice

GARNISH
orange-blossom water
rose water
finely chopped pistachio nuts

1 Follow the previous recipe to the end of stage 4.

2 Fold each pancake in half and pinch the edges together. Keep warm.

3 Heat the syrup, and drench the pancakes with it. Sprinkle with orange-blossom water, rose water and pistachio nuts, and serve piping hot.

UM M'ALI

Ali's mum's pud

Probably the best description of this thrifty dish is bread and butter pudding, Middle Eastern style. This particular version is from Egypt, and it uses scraps of dried filo pastry (*caleed gullash*). The Egyptians also use a type of cracker called *raqaq*, which is sold in packets. *Khoubiz* and other bread can also be used.

I have seen some pretty bizarre explanations of the name of this pudding, including an Irish connection (that it was the invention of one Mrs O'Malley, which has to be pure blarney!). *Um* (or *om*) in Arabic means 'mother' and Ali is as common a name as John. So the most likely literal translation is Ali's mum.

Serves 4

10–12oz (300–350g) filo or
  khoubiz bread
oil for deep-frying
2oz (50g) pine nuts
4oz (100g) walnuts, almonds or
  pistachio nuts, chopped (or a
  combination)
2oz (50g) sultanas or raisins
2oz (50g) dates, stoned and
  chopped

10–12 cloves
1 teaspoon powdered cinnamon
1 teaspoon ground green
  cardamom
1¾lb (800g) sweetened condensed
  milk (2 cans)
¼ pint (150ml) milk or cream

1 Pre-heat the oven to 400°F/200°C/Gas 6. Deep-fry the pieces of filo or bread. Drain, cool and break into small pieces.

2 Spread the pieces on the base of a baking dish about 10 × 8 inches (25 × 20cm).

3 Cover with the nuts, sultanas, dates, cloves, cinnamon and cardamom.

4 Warm (don't boil) the condensed milk and ordinary milk and cream together, then pour into the dish, ensuring that the other ingredients are completely covered.

5 Bake for 15–20 minutes, until the top forms a golden crust. Serve hot.

SEPHARDI TAMAR

Stuffed dates

Dates are synonymous with the Middle East, the date palm evoking images of deserts and oases. Dates grow profusely all over the Middle East, especially in Algeria, Tunisia, Iran and Israel. There are over 300 varieties and they range in colour from gold to red and dark brown. Two of the best varieties are *deglet noor* and *medjool*.

Dates are eaten fresh, used in cooking and they are preserved (as we know them best, a Christmas delicacy in those oval wooden boxes). In the Middle East they are eaten all year round at any meal, unaccompanied, with yoghurt, or stuffed with savoury or sweet fillings. In this particularly succulent Israeli recipe they make an excellent dessert.

Enough for 4–6 people

1 box preserved dates or, if you
   can get them, 16–20 fresh ripe
   dates

1 tablespoon sugar
1 teaspoon finely chopped
   pistachio nuts

FILLING
2 tablespoons ground almonds
$\frac{1}{2}$oz (15g) butter, softened

SYRUP
1 quantity 'atari (see page 167).

1 Carefully slit the dates down one side and remove the stones.

2 Make the filling by mixing the ingredients together. Use a little water to get a marzipan texture, then shape into pieces the size of date stones.

3 Insert into the dates.

4 Make the syrup following the recipe on page 167. (Any spare filling can be put in the syrup, or it can be frozen.)

5 Put the dates on a serving dish, and pour the hot syrup over them. Chill.

Rahat Lokum

Turkish Delight

Is there anyone in the world who doesn't know Turkish Delight, those gelatinous, squidgy, pastel-coloured squares dusted with icing sugar? Nothing has probably done more to promote a particular image of Turkey than this sweet – opulence, wealth, harems, voluptuous belly-dancers, and overweight sultans. It is an image which has nothing whatsoever to do with modern Turkey. The image endures, so too does Turkish Delight.

It can be made at home, but it is a recipe which needs patience and care to get it from a liquid to a gelatinous texture. The traditional ingredient for thickening is mastic, but you can use gelatine. Some recipes use cornflour, but this makes for a rather heavier texture. Many recipes require 2–3 hours of continuous stirring, but the following is, by those standards, quick and effort free.

Makes around 32 pieces

$\frac{1}{2}$ pint (300ml) water
1lb (450g) granulated white sugar
2 teaspoons lemon juice
$\frac{1}{8}$ teaspoon red food colouring
   (optional)

1oz (25g) powdered gelatine
2fl oz (50ml) water
$\frac{1}{2}$ teaspoon rose water
melted butter
icing sugar

1 Bring the ½ pint (300ml) water to the boil in a heavy pan, then add the sugar, lemon juice and colouring. Stir to ensure that it is well mixed.

2 Keep it boiling for 10–15 minutes. As it thickens, stir more often as and until it reduces into a thick but easily pourable syrup. Take off the heat and leave to cool for 10 minutes.

3 Dissolve the gelatine in the 2fl oz (50ml) water. Add it to the syrup, stir in well and bring it back to simmering. Add the rose water.

4 Select a small baking tin. I use a round tart tray about 6½ inches (17cm) in diameter and 1½ inches (4cm) deep. Brush with melted butter.

5 Pour the syrup into the tray and put it into the fridge for around 24 hours.

6 By then it should be firmly set like a jelly. Turn it out on to a board and sprinkle with icing sugar. Cut into pieces about 1 inch (2.5cm) square. Keep in an airtight box, where they will last for a few weeks.

Note: Alternatives include the addition of green food colouring in place of red, and chopped pistachio nuts added at stage 3. Or omit food colouring and rose water and add 1 teaspoon of vanilla essence.

LOSE HILOO

Sugared almonds

These whole almonds, fried in butter and dusted in sugar, are exceedingly effective served cold as a garnish to sweet dishes or on their own with coffee or tea. They are simplicity itself to make. Any nuts can be used this way – almonds are particularly suitable.

Serves 4

2oz (50g) butter
8oz (225g) shelled whole almonds
caster sugar

1 Melt the butter in a wok or frying pan.

2 Add the almonds and stir-fry for 2–3 minutes, turning them frequently.

3 Strain the butter away, keeping it for future use.

4 Allow the almonds to cool, then dust with caster sugar.

5 Store in an air-tight tin/jar, where they will last for months.

CHAPTER · 12

AFTER THE MEAL

IN A culture where alcohol is either forbidden, severely disapproved of, or tolerated, other beverages take its place. They always appear after the meal, and indeed they appear endlessly throughout the day.

COFFEE

In many Middle Eastern countries, coffee is the favoured brew. Traditionally it is very strong and thick, with a layer of sludge at the bottom.

Coffee is now a world-wide phenomenon, but it was the Arabs who discovered it growing wild in Abyssinia (now Ethiopia), the African country across the narrow waters of the Red Sea from Saudi Arabia. Roots and berries had been infused in boiling water since ancient times to produce hot brews, so it is not surprising that coffee was subjected to this process. Exactly when this first took place and how the process of roasting raw green beans before grinding and brewing them was conceived, is lost to time. The Arabs imported Abyssinian coffee into the ancient Yemeni port of Al Mukha. Most researchers agree that coffee was being cultivated in the area by AD 550, 100 years before Islam. The harvest was small, and the brew confined to a few devotees. That coffee was a powerful stimulant was recognized by the early fanatical followers of Mohammed, who regarded it as unfavourably as they did alcohol. But it escaped prohibition, and indeed it was later generations of Moslem monks, the dervishes, who made coffee drinking ritualistic, significant and permanent.

Despite the rapid spread of Arab power over the next few centuries, coffee drinking was unknown outside southern Arabia. This was possibly because of the importance it had achieved in Islamic religious ceremony, particularly in Mecca. There it must have been tasted by Moslem pilgrims who flocked to Mecca from all parts of the vast Islamic world to pay hommage to Mohammed. But it took 1,000 years for coffee to become known to the world outside Arabia. With the shift of the balance of power to Turkey in the fifteenth century, it was inevitable that coffee would follow. The honours of introducing the infusion to the Ottoman court fell, it is said, to a Syrian spice merchant. The Arab *q'ahwah* became the Turkish *khave*. It became immediately popular all over the Ottoman Empire and within a century it was widely consumed from the Maghreb to Armenia. Its introduction to Europe was equally spectacular. The Christian Church was at first as suspicious of coffee as the early Moslems and it took a papal edict for it to be accepted.

It was the Turkish ambassador to France who created a sensation in 1669 when he offered coffee to his guests, thereby introducing coffee to Europe for the first time. And it was an Armenian who just three years later opened the first coffee shop in Paris. Within a decade coffee shops were opened in every fashionable European city. Business was done there and they became the forerunners of banks, finance houses and gentlemen's clubs. Coffee reached the New World during the eighteenth century, and most of the world's coffee now comes from South America.

Arab and Turkish coffees are identical in preparation. The traditional bean is the *mocha* (named after the port of Al Mukha). This is a dark, strong, full-bodied coffee, ground to a very fine powder. Households all over the Middle East have coffee on the go during all their waking hours. Its serving remains as much a ritual as it was hundreds of years ago. Now it is one of hospitality rather than of religion.

The ritual begins with the roasting, cooling and pulverizing of the coffee bean – it must be done freshly either at home or by a coffee merchant in a *tahrini* (coffee grinder). It is brewed in a purpose-made brass or enamelled pot, a vessel with a narrow neck and long handle which holds between one and six servings of coffee. The cups themselves are tiny, smaller than demi-tasse measures, with or without handles. In formal situations, at table, for example, the coffee is poured by the host, the first cup is passed to the senior guest, then the remaining cups are passed round the table anticlockwise. The host refills the cups in the order they were served until the drinkers indicate by a wiggle of the cup that they have had enough.

The first time a Westerner has this kind of coffee it can come as a surprise. It is always taken black and the coffee powder is not filtered into the cup. The result is that about one-third of the liquid is a totally unpalatable sludge which settles on the bottom of the cup. One therefore sips only the top half or so of one's cup, which in reality is only a mouthful or two. For this reason one is expected to drink two or three cups. To drink less is an insult to the host (but to drink more will keep you awake all night, it is very strong indeed!). It is also normally brewed with a lot of sugar, although the sweetness index can be to the drinker's taste – *ziyadda* or *hilou* is extra sweet, *mazboutah* or *madhbout* is just a little sugar, and *murrah* is without sugar. Sugarless coffee symbolizes times of unhappiness – it is taken for example by all participants at a funeral.

Coffee Western-style is now becoming almost as popular in the Arab world as the traditional coffee. The term *q'ahwah Fransawi* (literally French coffee) covers everything from filtered grounds to instant coffee.

Q'AHWAH ARABIYA

Arab coffee

This is the original Middle Eastern infusion brewed with the aromatic flavour of cardamom.

1 The strength of the brew is up to you, but it is normally 2 teaspoons per cup for strong, and 1 teaspoon for medium. Add sugar to taste in the ratio of 1 teaspoon per cup sweet, $\frac{1}{2}$ teaspoon medium sweet, and so on. Finally add ground green cardamom, $\frac{1}{2}$ teaspoon per cup. Mix these ingredients.

2 Into a saucepan, measure the exact quantity of water you intend to drink in one of the cups you will use (six full measures for six cups), and bring to the boil.

3 Add the ingredients from stage 1, and bring back to the boil. Simmer for around 10 minutes.

4 Bring back to the boil, and serve at once to ensure that each cup gets a similar amount of 'grounds'.

5 Allow a minute or two for the 'grounds' to settle before drinking.

Q'SHR

Yemeni coffee

Prepare exactly as for Arabic coffee, but use $\frac{1}{4}$ teaspoon of ground ginger per cup in place of the cardamom.

KHAVE TURKI

Turkish coffee

This is the coffee many of us will be familiar with from Turkish restaurants (in Greek restaurants it is called Greek coffee!). Spices are omitted, and the brewing method is lighter, creating a topping of froth.

1 Use the same measures of ground Turkish coffee to determine strength. Sugar strengths are the same too, but the Turkish terms are *sekerli*, very sweet, *orta*, medium sweet, and *sade*, sugarless.

2 Put the measured water into a pan along with the coffee and sugar.

3 Bring to the boil. It will froth. Take the pan off the heat, and allow to cool for a minute.

4 Repeat stage 3 twice more then serve the coffee at once, ensuring that each cup gets an equal amount of 'grounds'. Try to pour a little froth (*wijih*) into each cup.

5 Allow the 'grounds' to settle in the cup for a minute or two before drinking.

Q'AHWAH M'GREBI

Maghreb coffee

Follow either the Arab or Turkish method. In place of cardamom, add $\frac{1}{4}$ teaspoon powdered cinnamon. Just before serving add 1 drop orange-blossom water per person.

TEA

In some Middle Eastern countries tea is drunk much more than coffee, especially in Iran, Armenia and surprisingly, perhaps, Turkey. Despite their imagined predilection for coffee, tea drinking in Turkey far outweighs that of coffee. It also does in the Maghreb, where they enjoy the delectable *chai bi na'na*, the mint tea originally invented in Morocco, but now found all over the Middle East. *Haiganon tey*, Armenian tea, includes cloves and cinnamon, whilst *chaiy turki*, Turkish tea, relies on the fragrance of the tea itself.

CHAI BI NA'NA

Moroccan mint tea

The Berbers have been drinking an infusion with fresh mint since they first inhabited the Maghreb thousands of years ago. It took the British to make the only significant change the brew had known in its long life. After the start of the Crimean War, many of the British tea traders' central European markets disappeared overnight. Desperate to sell their surplus tea the traders tried, amongst other places, North Africa. They found the Maghrebi mint brew and suggested that tea be added to it and amazingly it became an instant success.

It is a wonderfully refreshing drink – especially on a summer's afternoon. The teas that blend most sympathetically with mint are green Chinese teas such as oolong, jasmine or green gunpowder. Spearmint is the mint widely used to make Moroccan tea, but other varieties, especially peppermint, are equally interesting (see Herbs Glossary).

Makes 4 cups

approx. 1¼ pints (750ml) water
3–4 teaspoons tea leaves
20–30 spearmint leaves
4 sprigs mint

1 Boil the water in a kettle.

2 Warm the teapot. Put the tea and mint leaves in and add the boiling water.

3 Leave it to brew for 2 or 3 minutes.

4 During stage 3, warm tumblers by rinsing in hot water.

5 Put one sprig of mint into each tumbler.

6 Pour the tea into each tumbler through a strainer. It is normal to add sugar lumps to the teapot, but it can be added to the tumbler to taste after pouring.

HAIGANAN TEY

Armenian tea

Cinnamon is used in this Caucasian tea to produce a sweetish, very fragrant infusion. They make it with or without tea, using cinnamon sticks or cassia bark (*dartchinov*). This recipe uses cinnamon quills and a delicate smoky tea such as Chinese keemun, lapsang souchong or fan yong. No milk is used.

Makes 4 cups

approx. 1¼ pints (750ml) water
6 cloves
4 cinnamon quills, about 2½ inches
   (6 cm) long
3–4 teaspoons tea leaves

1 Follow the mint tea recipe on page 175, using cloves and cinnamon instead of the mint, to the end of stage 4.

2 Pour the tea into a tumbler through a strainer. Sweeten to taste.

CHAIY TURKI

Turkish tea

Tea drinking probably arrived in Turkey at the time of the Ottomans over 400 years ago. Their tea was imported from Persia until plantations were established in the Black Sea area under British supervision about 100 years ago. Contrary to popular supposition, much more tea is drunk in Turkey than coffee. It is always on hand in special teapots and is served without milk in special small tumblers.

Turkish tea is sometimes obtainable in the West. Otherwise use any tea of your choice – Assam from India will, for example, give a strong reddish brew, whilst jasmine tea from China is very delicately scented with jasmine blossoms.

Makes 4 tumblers

approx. 1¼ pints (750ml) water
4–6 teaspoons tea leaves

Follow the recipe for mint tea on page 175, omitting the mint.

GLOSSARIES

THIS section is sub-divided into herb and spice sections followed by a general glossary. The purpose of the general glossary is to enable the user to identify Middle Eastern ingredients, techniques and terms used in this book. All words are Arabic or English unless otherwise stated.

For the definition of a particular dish and its recipe please consult the index at the end of this book.

HERB GLOSSARY

(see also page 32)

Basil (rayhan, reeyan) *Largish flat green leaf*
A most fragrant and delightful herb, easily obtainable in the West.

Chervil *Delicate feathery leaf*
A native to the area, it has a parsley/aniseed flavour. Used as a pretty garnish.

Coriander (kazbara, kuzbarah) *Flat green leaf*
Widely used in Middle Eastern cooking. The leaves are called *kuzbarah khadra* (fresh coriander) to distinguish them from the seeds (see Spice Glossary). Named after the Greek word '*korus*', a bedbug, apparently because the leaf's slightly foetid smell resembles these pests.

Cress (barbeen) *Dark green leaf*
Of the mustard family. Resembles watercress but with much smaller leaves. Used in Iranian stews where it is called *shahat*, and all over the Gulf, both in cooking and salads. There are many other varieties of cress. *Jargeer* is sharp tasting.

Dill (shabth) *Feathery blue-green leaf*
An ideal garnish, its aniseed flavour also enhances meat, vegetable or rice dishes.

Fennel (shummar) *Feathery leaf, mid-green in colour*
Used as dill.

Garlic Chives (tareh) *Flat-bladed leaf*
Native to and used in Iranian cooking. Its leaves are larger than ordinary chives, but it has, as its name states, a garlicky taste. Also called Chinese chives.

Marjoram (samaq itrah) *sweet-scented flower, small leaves*
Powerful aroma but easily lost if overcooked. It is added fresh to the dish a couple of minutes before serving.

Marjoram, Wild (rigani) *Bitter-sweet flower and small leaves*
Related to marjoram, and there are several varieties. Used in Greek cooking to flavour items such as kebabs. It is virtually impossible to obtain in Britain.

Melokhia *Spinach-like darkish green leaf*
Member of the jute family virtually exclusive to Egypt, and rarely found fresh elsewhere. A dried substitute lacks flavour. The Egyptians use it to flavour many savoury dishes. Its most celebrated Egyptian use is in one of the country's national dishes – the soup called appropriately *melokhia*.

Mint (na'na) *Bright green leaf*
Various varieties grow everywhere. The most common type to be used in cooking is spearmint. Always best fresh, it is used in a variety of ways – stewed in the mint tea of Morocco (see page 175), fried and added to Arab soups, dried in stews and chutneys, and fresh in salads. It is one of the most distinctive tastes of the Middle East. *Na'na* literally means 'the gift of Allah'.

Parsley (bagdunis) *Flat green leaf*
In the Middle East most parsley is flat-leaved rather than the Western curly leaved variety. It tastes the same.

Purslane (bakli, baglah, farfhin) *Green fleshy leaf growing on red stalk*
Spinach-like vegetable which grows in the wild and is cultivated. Particularly popular in the Levant, where it is notable in *fatoush*, a fresh salad containing toasted bread. It used to be popular in Elizabethan England in stews, but is hard to come by in the West today.

Rosemary (hasa il-ban or iklil bi jabal) *Silvery-grey spiky tough leaf*
Particularly popular in Morocco (where it appears in ras-el-hanout). A very aromatic, distinctive herb.

Sage (maramiyah) *Oblong green leaf*
Popular in kebab marinades and in salads, sage is fairly powerful and should be used sparingly.

Thyme (za'atar) *Small grey-green leaf*
Widely used as a background flavour in casseroles, and this too is powerful.

SPICE GLOSSARY

(see also page 33)

Allspice (bahar hah hilu) *Round dark brown seeds*
The allspice seed looks like a large peppercorn. It fooled its discoverer, Columbus, who located it in Jamaica and named it pimento or Jamaican pepper. The confusion remains to this day. It is not a member of the pepper family and 'allspice' describes it better. Its taste is quite aromatic, resembling a combination of cinnamon, clove, ginger, nutmeg and pepper itself. This conveniently packages in one item the taste enjoyed all over the Middle East, and it is therefore widely used there.

Aniseed (yansoon) *Small grey-green seeds*
Native to the area. One of the first spices to be cultivated in Egypt. It appears in savoury and sweet dishes and is fundamental to the spirits *ouzo* and *raki*. Its main essential oil is anethole, also present in the non-related fennel and star anise.

Barberry (zereshk) *Red-brown berries*
The berries are dried whole and resemble currants in texture and colour but not in taste. They are very sour, and are used whole in Iranian cooking.

Bay Leaves (waraq il ghar) *Green spear-shaped leaves*
Native to Asia Minor. Used in the same way as in the West to flavour stews, etc, fresh or dried, especially in Greece and Turkey.

Caraway (karawya) *Small, thin, black seeds*
Has been used for over 5,000 years as a cooking spice, in pastries, savouries, sweets and salads.

Cardamom, Green (hayl or hab han) *Green pod cases containing aromatic black seeds*
Native to India and brought back by the Middle Eastern traders in the centuries BC, it is an expensive spice, but is widely used, especially in Arabia and Iran to flavour Arab coffee.

Cassia (darseen) and Cinnamon (kirfee) *Brown bark pieces or quills*
The inner bark of evergreen trees closely related but from different species. Both are used for the sweetness the bark imparts. Cassia is native to China,

is cheaper and generally more robust. Cinnamon is native to Sri Lanka, and was taken to China and later traded to the Middle East.

Chilli (bisbas, fel fel or filfil) *Fleshy green pods*
Members of the capsicum family, which turn red when ripe. There are over 1,500 species ranging in size from tiny to large and in heat grading from volcanic to mild. Native to Latin America and not introduced to the Arab lands until the sixteenth century, until when Indian pepper was the primary heat source. They are now a part of the way of life in some countries.

Clove (habahan, kabsh kurnful) *Dark brown 'nail'-shaped (from the Latin 'clavus' meaning nail)*
The rounded 'head' of the clove is an unopened flower bud. Cropping is slow and expensive, and if mistimed and the flower opens, the clove is useless. Native to the Moluccan Islands in Indonesia (although few grow there now), they were a major trading crop in medieval times. Today they are mainly harvested in Zanzibar, Madagascar and Grenada. One of the few spices to have remained in constant use in Britain, both in cooking (apples for example) and medicine (the oil is a soother at the dentist). They have a great application in Middle Eastern cooking.

Coriander (kazbara) *Round pale brown seeds (see also page 177)*
The seeds of the coriander plant are infrequently used whole in Middle Eastern cooking, but ground they are used in many recipes. They impart a sweetish, slightly musky taste, quite unlike fresh coriander leaves.

Cummin (kammun) *small greenish seeds*
Native to upper Egypt and the Levant, cummin has been found in the Pyramids. One of the most popular spices, especially so in Morocco and Tunisia, where it is the only spice used in some dishes.

Cummin, Black (habet el baraka) *small, thin, black seeds*
In appearance similar to caraway with which they are often confused, but their taste is much less sweet and more astringent. Used in rice dishes.

Fenugreek (hilbah, hulba) *Golden brown nugget-like seeds*
An Asian native, long since brought westwards, the name derives from the Latin *'fenum graecum'*, Greek leaves. It is, however, scarcely used in Greek cooking, and that derivation probably refers to the time when the Greek empire extended as far as India, where the seed and its leaves are an important curry ingredient. Fenugreek is powerful, and an acquired taste, being bitter when raw, but less so when cooked. It is not universally popular in the Middle East. Iranian cooking uses both seed and leaf, and the Iraqis use the seed in certain dishes. One speciality that does use it is *pastourma*, dried salt beef. It is ground into a paste and rubbed on to the beef prior to drying. This same dish is found in Turkey and Armenia

(*aboukht*). In the Yemen, the speciality *hilbeh*, named after the spice itself, is a very hot dip containing fenugreek and coriander (see page 50). It is also baked in bread (see page 154).

Ginger (zanjabil) *Irregularly shaped root covered with dry, parchment-coloured skin*

This rhizome, native to the South East Asian jungle, is now grown in India and many other tropical countries. The fresh root travels well, keeps for months and is now well known in the greengrocers of the West. Dry or powdered can be used as a substitute, and it was this form that the Arabs first traded with Chinese merchants. It is in fact not used extensively in Middle Eastern cooking.

Mahlab

Mahlab has no English translation and is only found in the Middle East. The spice is obtained from the seed of a black cherry originally native to Syria. The seed is opened and discarded after the kernel, a pale brown seed the size of a peppercorn, the *mahlab* itself, is extracted. It is always sold whole and must be freshly ground to retain its sweet, aromatic properties and it is only used in baking. The Arab bun *ka'ak* or the Armenian *choerig* biscuit, and other cakes and breads containing *mahleb*, have a unique flavour.

Nutmeg (jawaz a'tib) *Hard, round, pale, brown ball*

Native to South East Asia, it was introduced to the West by the earliest Arab and Chinese traders. It is a kernel around which the lattice-like mace grows, the outer case being a pithy green fruit. Nutmeg is widely used in the Middle East, especially in the spice mix *baharat*.

Paprika (filfil hilu) *Bright red ground pepper*

Made from red capsicum bell peppers, the Arabic meaning literally 'pepper-sweet'. It is used for colouring as much as flavouring.

Pepper, Black (filfil aswan) *Whole black corns or ground*

An important spice, well-known worldwide.

Pepper, White (filfil beida) *Whole white corns or ground*

As well known as black pepper.

Pomegranate (ruman, anar) *Deep reddish-brown sticky seeds*

Native to Iran and much relished there. The soft round fruit is eaten raw with salt or sugar. Both flesh and seeds are used in Iranian cooking as a souring agent. In the Levant, the seeds, fresh or dried, are compressed to produce a dark brown syrup (grenadine) used for flavouring foods, or, with plentiful sugar, as a drink (especially favoured in the Gulf). The dry seeds are also used as a garnish. Pomegranate has always been greatly respected. Genesis claims it to be the tree of life (it was more than likely the apple in the garden of Eden), and the Koran states that the consumption of pomegranate represses thoughts of envy. At the Turkish wedding ceremony, a custom from ancient times is to throw a whole ripe pomegranate to the ground. The number of seeds spilling out tells how many children the couple will have.

Poppy Seed *Tiny blue or cream-coloured seeds*
There are many species of poppy, including the opium varieties. Poppy seeds contain no opium. The blue or cream seeds are from different species, but the taste is the same. They are primarily used to garnish bread and cakes. On the Jewish holiday Purim, which celebrates the failure of an ancient Persian invasion, a triangular pastry, *hamantaschen*, containing poppy seeds is the speciality of the day. The Egyptians at the times of the Pharaohs favoured poppy seeds, and the Greeks fed their Olympic athletes on honey and poppy seed cakes.

Saffron (za'faran) *Deep orange/crimson threads*
The threads are the stigma of a particular species of crocus. Three grow in each crocus and they must be gently hand-picked at exactly the right moment of ripeness, then dried as soon as possible. The method of cropping cannot be automated and this, coupled with the fact that it takes 225,000 stigmas, or 75,000 crocuses to make 1lb (450g) of saffron, makes it the world's most expensive spice. It originated in Turkey, and now grows in Iran, Kashmir and Spain, where the Arabs planted it in the tenth century. The very word saffron is derived from the Arabic *za'faran* meaning yellow, and it is as a fragrant colourer that it is mostly used. Although it is used in dishes involving prolonged cooking, it is wasted in this role – all its flavour is lost.

Sesame (sum sum) *Small, flat, round, pale cream seeds*
These come in other colours, including red, brown and black, the latter being used in Chinese cooking. But it is the cream seed (called white) which is so widely used in the Middle East, where it is indigenous. Today it is pressed into an oil, included in baking, but its most widespread use is in the mixture *tahine*.

Sumak (sumaq) *Dried very dark red berries*
The berries from the *sumaq* tree, native to Iran, are used whole or ground as a souring agent in cooking in all sorts of meat or vegetable dishes. It is also used in fish dishes, which can lead to confusion, as the Arabic word for fish is *samak* (singular) and *sameq* (plural), and the dish *sameq al harrah* is fish baked with chilli, tahine, garlic, pine nuts and *sumaq*.

Turmeric (kurkum) *Fine yellow powder*
Native to South Asia, turmeric is a rhizome which, like ginger, can be cooked fresh. Turmeric is normally encountered ground, though, and is used primarily for giving colour. It is bitter, so is used sparingly, and although recipe books claim it can be substituted for saffron, it will give

neither the brightness and individuality of colour nor the fragrance of saffron. Turmeric is widely used in Indian curry (the Arabic *kurkum* could be another derivative of the word 'curry'). In the Middle East it is used in countries as far apart as Morocco and Iran.

GENERAL GLOSSARY

A

Aadou – Mezzeh (Tunisia)

Aash – Iranian soup (Persian)

Abgusht – Meat cooked with yoghurt and spices (Persian)

Ads – Lentils

Ageen – Pastry

Aish or Aiysh – Bread (Egyptian)

Ajja – Omelette

Alya – Cooking fat made from rendered sheep's tail (Arab). *Kuyruk yahi* (Turkish)

Anar – Pomegranate

Arak – Alcholic beverage made from grape flavoured with aniseed. Widely enjoyed where Moslem laws do not apply. Called *raki* in Turkey, *oghi* in Armenia, *ouzo* in Greece

Arnhab – Rabbit

Assafeer – Quail

Assal – Honey

Atari – Syrup

B

Bagdunis – Parsley

Bahar – Mixture of four spices (clove, cinnamon, nutmeg and pepper)

Bahar Hah Hilu – Allspice

Baharat or Bharat – The above mixture, plus coriander, cummin, pepper and paprika

Baidh – Egg

Bakli or Baglah – Purslane

Bamia – Okra

Bamir – Cheese made from milk curds (Armenian) similar to Indian *panir* and Turkish *peynir*. Usually milk of sheep or cow, occasionally goat or mare

Barbeen – Cress

Basal – Onion

Basterma – Spicy dried beef (Armenia)

Bataresh – Salty Egyptian fish roe

Batellu – Veal

Batt – Duck

Bekmez – Thick grape juice syrup

Berenje – Rice (Iran)

Bhar – See *Bahar*

Bisbas – Chilli

Booza-booza – Ice cream

Borani – Iranian salad with yoghurt

Bourgouri or Burghul – Wheat is husked, partly cooked, dried, then ground to three grades – coarse for stuffing and rice dishes, medium for fillings and fine for salads. Burghul originated with the earliest civilizations in the Levant and was probably mankind's first processed food.

C

Couscous – Semolina product

Couscousière – Couscous cooking pot

D

Dajaj – Chicken

Damassa – Egyptian utensil for cooking *ful* (beans)

Danee – Lamb

Darseen – Cassia

Dersa – Hot, spicy Algerian sauce

Dibbis Rhumas or Dibs Romana – Syrup made from pomegranate used to flavour savoury dishes (Lebanese)

Djej – Chicken

Dolma – Stuffed vegetable (Turkish), dolmades (Greek), *dolmeh* (Persian)

Doner – Type of kebab found all over the Middle East but originating in Turkey

Dukkah – Dry spice/nut/herb mixtures

E

Eggah – Omelette (Egyptian)

F

Fakhid – Leg (of lamb)
Farfhin – Purslane
Fel Fel – Chilli
Fel Fel Sudani – Hot spicy sauce from Morocco
Felafel – Chickpea croquette
Ferakh – Chicken
Ferakh Hadjal – Partridge
Feta – Goat cheese found in Greece, Turkey and Iran
Filfil Ahmar – Chilli pepper, red
Filfil Aswah – Black pepper
Filfil Beida – White pepper
Filfil Hilu – Paprika
Filo, also Fila, Phila, Phyllo and Yufka – Very thinly rolled Greek pastry (see page 66)
Firinda – Baked (Turkish)
Firri – Baby chicken or poussin
Ful – Broad beans (Egypt)
Ful Medamis – Small, round, brown beans, used to make the Egyptian 'national dish'
Ful Nabed – Large, flat, round, broad beans with a pale brown skin. The actual beans are white and are used in *bassarah* and *ta'amiah* (Egyptian)

G

Gamar id-Din – Paste of cooked apricot. When used to make a drink it is called *sharab gamar id-din*
Gambari – Shrimps/prawns
Gamil – Camel
Girfar – Cinnamon
Gul Suyu – Rosewater (Turkish)
Guvech – Cooking style where ingredients are baked in and eaten from a pottery dish (Turkish/Armenian)

H

Habahan – Clove
Hab Han – Green cardamom
Hab Hilu – Allspice
Habash – Turkey
Habb – Husked wheat kernels

Habet el Baraka – Black cummin
Halal – Moslem food preparation laws (see pages 21 and 78)
Halawal or Halva – A sweet or dessert
Haleeb – Milk
Haloumi – Salty cheese usually from milk, goat or sheep, sometimes cow (Lebanese). *Hallumi* (Greek), *hellim* (Turkish)
Hamaan – Pigeon
Hamindas – Eggs cooked in Israeli *cholent* (stew). *Hamine* similar in Egypt
Hasa il-Ban – Rosemary
Hayl – Green cardamom
Heloo or Hilu – Sweet
Hilba or Hilbeh or Hulba – Spice dip
Hoummus or Humous – Chickpea (garbanzo bean), first cultivated in Egypt
Hout – Fish (Maghreb)
Humir – Tamarind
Huwmara – White flour

I

Iggah – Omelette
Istakoz – Lobster (Turkish)
Iklil bi Jabal – Rosemary

J

Jawaz a 'Tib – Nutmeg

K

Kabsh Kurnful – Cloves
Kafta – Meatballs (Iranian)
Kammun – Cummin
Kandouz – Beef
Karawya – Caraway
Kazbara – Coriander
K'dra – Cooking with fat or *samneh* (Moroccan), see *Mqali*
Kebab or Kabab, Kabaub, Kobob – Literally means cooked meat. The Turks perfected marination and other methods. Doner means to turn, and shish, *sis*, *sheesh*, *sheik* means skewer in Turkish. Shashlik means meat and vegetables on a skewer (Armenian), *hasina* is the same thing in Persian, and *shami* is a ground meat rissole (Syrian)
Kemia – Mezzeh (Algeria)
Khal – Vinegar
Kharouf – Lamb

Kharub – Carob. Pods of an evergreen tree dried in the sun then enjoyed for their chocolate taste. Available in powdered form

Khdar or Akhdar – Green

Khadra – Fresh

Khashkar – Brown flour

Khoubiz or Khobz, etc – Standard Arabian bread

Khozi – Pork

Khudar – Vegetables

Khulinjan – Galingale

Kibbeh or Kibbi – Vegetables stuffed with a mixture of burghul and meat

Kirfee – Cinnamon

Kiymeh – Minced (meat)

Kofteh or Kofta – See *Kafta*

Kosher – Jewish food preparation laws (see pages 12, 21 and 78)

Kunafeh – Shredded filo dough for making *kadayif* (see page 162)

Kurfee – Cinnamon

Kurkum – Turmeric

Kuzbarah – Coriander

L

La Kama – Spice mix (Moroccan)

Laban – Yoghurt

Labnah – Cheesy yoghurt

Laham – Meat

Laham Meshwi – Cooked meat

Lawz – Almonds

Limu Omani or Loomi or Noomi – Dried whole limes, or ground limes used to give sour taste to savoury dishes (Iranian).

Loze – Almonds

M

Magli – Boiled

Mahlab – A spice

M'ahmar – Red

M'ali – Fried

Mansaaf – Bedouin banquet dish involving a whole roast lamb and rice. The eyes are regarded as the main delicacy

Maramiyah – Sage

M'ashi(ya) or Mahchi – Stuffed

Masgeof – To grill or broil

Mashwi – All types of meat

Matbook – Cooked

Maward – Rose water (Arabic)

Mazaher – Orange blossoms distilled in water. Used in delicate meat and rice dishes, sweets and in coffee

Mechoui or M'choui – To grill (Arabic), grill whole sheep (Maghreb)

Meffened or M'fenned – A topping (see Chapter Four)

Megli – Fried

Mehammer – Fried

Mekali – Pickled items in vinegar

Melokhia – Green plant shoots, a bit spinach-like, used in Egyptian dishes

Mergez or Mergues, Merguvez – Hot, spicy, dry sausage made from mutton or goat and flavoured with harissa (Tunisian/Algerian)

Meshwi – All types of meat

Mezzeh – Mixed hors-d'oeuvres

Mikhatel – Pickled items in vinegar

Mishi – Stuffed

Mishmish or Mechmach – Apricot. Eaten fresh, ripe and juicy, of course, but it makes other appearances. Dried, it is one of the sweet-sour agencies in Iranian meat dishes. It is also made into a paste which is used in cookery or to make drinks. During Ramadan many people drink *sharab gamar-id-din* made from this paste to break the fast

Mishshi – Stuffed vegetables (see *Kibbeh*)

Mishwi – All types of meat

Missabek – Stewed

Mistika – Mastic. Edible resin (sap) from an evergreen shrub used especially in meat dishes to enhance flavours and to bind meat in kebabs

Mqali – Cooking with olive oil (Moroccan), see *k'dra*

Mqali – Pickled items in vinegar

Mugaddra – Lentils

Muhammer – Sweet rice

Mussir – Wild garlic

N

Na'na – Mint

Noomi – See *Limu Omani*

P

Pastrouma – Spicy dried beef (Israeli)

Peynir – See *Bamir*

Pilich – Chicken (Turkish)

Pitta – The well-known unleavened bread with a pocket

Plaki – Cooking style. Fish or vegetable cooked in olive oil with herbs, tomato and garlic. It originated in Byzantine times and is still eaten in Greece, Turkey and Armenia

Pourgouri – See *Bourgouri*

Q

Qali – Vinegar

R

Raki – See *Arak*

Ras el Hanout – Celebrated Moroccan spice mix

Rayhan or Reeyan – Basil

Reuchta – Noodles. The word means 'thread' in Persian and Arabic. Found in the Maghreb, there are two styles – *jda* (very thin) and *noissara* ($\frac{1}{2}$ inch/1 cm squares)

Rghaif – Pancake dough (Maghreb)

Rigani – Type of wild marjoram

Ruman – Pomegranate

S

Sabzi – Vegetables or herbs (Iranian)

Samneh or Smen – Clarified butter

Samak – Fish

Samaq Itrah – Marjoram

Sbar – Spiced with tamarind

Shabth – Dill

Shorba – Soup

Shummar – Fennel

Smen – Clarified butter

Snawbar or Snorbeh – Pine nuts

Soudjuk – Dried sausage

Soumanate – Quail

Summak – Dried berries

Sum Sum – Sesame

Susmeyagli – See *Smen*

T

Ta'amiah – Rissole-shaped croquette made from *ful nabed* beans. The Egyptian version of *felafel*

Tagine – Type of slow-cooked stew (Moroccan)

Tahini or Tahina or Tahine – A paste made from ground sesame seeds and olive oil

Ta'leya – A garnish of onion and garlic fried in olive oil used in Egypt

Tamar – Date

Tamer Hind – Tamarind (literally means Indian date)

Tarama – The roe of red or grey mullet

Taratoor – Sauce or dip

Tareh – Garlic chives

Tatli Surubu – Sugar syrup

Tereyagli – Butter (Turkish)

Thawn or Tum – Garlic

Tiin – Fig. The fig is mentioned in the Bible and is a popular fruit in the Middle East. There are hundreds of varieties with skin colours of all hues. The flesh is usually blood coloured, with a multitude of seeds, and undoubtedly taste best fresh from the tree.

Tmar – Date

Turlu – Casserole using (usually) vegetables only (Turkish/Armenian)

W

Waraq il Ghar – Bay leaf

Warkah or Ouarka, Malsougva or Dioul – Tracing-paper-thin transparent pastry (Morocco)

Y

Yansoon – Aniseed

Yahni – Arab method of cooking. Meat or vegetables braised in oil with onion, then simmered with water to make a stock. Used from Egypt to Iran (and a derivative *yakni*, in India)

Yershig – Dried sausage (Armenian)

Z

Za'atar – A blend of powdered herbs, especially thyme with marjoram, *sumak* and (sometimes) roasted sesame seeds

Za'faran – Saffron

Zanjabil – Ginger

Za'tar – Thyme

Zaytun, Zayı or Zeytun – Olive.

Zeytunagli – Olive oil

Zereshk – Barberry, see Spice Glossary

Zhug – Spice mixture (Yemeni)

APPENDIX 1

THE CURRY CLUB

Pat Chapman has always had a deep-rooted interest in spicy food, curry in particular, and over the years he has built up a huge pool of information which he felt could be usefully passed on to others. He conceived the idea of forming an organization for this purpose.

Since it was founded in January 1982, The Curry Club has built up a membership of several thousands. It has a marchioness, some lords and ladies, a captain or two of industry, generals, admirals and air marshals (not to mention a sprinkling of ex-colonels), and it has celebrity names – actresses, politicians, rock stars and sportsmen. It has an airline (Air India), a former RN warship (HMS *Hermes*) and a hotel chain (the Taj group). It has members on every continent and a good number of Asian members too, but by and large the membership is a typical cross-section of the Great British Public, ranging in age from teenage to dotage, in occupation from refuse collectors to receivers, high street traders to high court judges, and tax inspectors to taxi drivers. There are students and pensioners, millionaires and unemployed ... thousands of people who have just one thing in common – a love of curry and spicy foods.

Members receive a bright and colourful magazine three times a year, which has regular features on curry and the curry lands. It includes news items, recipes, reports on restaurants, picture features and contributions from members and professionals alike. The information is largely concerned with curry but by popular demand it now includes regular input on other exotic and spicy cuisines such as that of the Middle East. The Club has produced a wide selection of publications, including the books listed on page 2, all published by Piatkus. There is also a cookery video.

Obtaining ingredients required for Indian, Oriental and Middle Eastern cooking can be difficult, but The Curry Club makes it easy with its well-established and efficient mail order service. Over 500 items are stocked, including spices, pickles, pastes, dry foods, tinned foods, gift items, publications and specialist kitchen and tableware.

On the social side, the Club organizes regular activities all over the UK. These range from monthly 'nights' in London and specific 'nights' elsewhere, enabling members to meet the Club organizers, discuss queries, buy supplies and enjoy spicy snacks or meals. The Club also holds day and residential weekend cookery courses, gourmet nights to selected restaurants, and similar enjoyable outings.

Top of the list is our regular Curry Club Gourmet Trip to India and other spicy countries. We take a small group of curry enthusiasts to the chosen country and tour the incredible sights, in between sampling the delicious foods of each region.

If you'd like to know more, write to **Pat Chapman, The Curry Club, PO Box 7, Haslemere, Surrey GU27 1EP. Telephone 01428 658327.**

APPENDIX 2

THE STORE CUPBOARD

Below are listed all the specialist ingredients used in this book. Items marked * are used in three or less recipes. The list may look formidable, but all these items will keep for a good long time if stored correctly (best in airtight containers in a damp-free, dark, out-of-sunlight, place). And even if you need to buy everything the cost is relatively low. The items that are available by post from The Curry Club are those which state quantities (see Appendix 1 for address). The quantities are either metric or imperial depending on the manufacturers.

Whole Spices
Allspice 30 g
*Aniseed 45 g
*Barberry (zereshk) 25 g
Bay leaf 3 g
Cardamom, green 30 g
*Caraway 30 g
*Cassia bark 30 g
Cinnamon quill 20 g
Cloves 20 g
*Coriander seeds 45 g
*Cummin, black 25 g
Cummin, white 60 g
Fennel seed 25 g
*Fenugreek leaf 18 g
Fenugreek seed 40 g
*Mahlab 20 g
Mint, dried 40 g
*Mustard seed, black 60g
Nutmeg 30 g
*Pomegranate seed 30 g
*Poppy seed, white 50 g
Saffron 0.5 g
Sesame seed, white 50 g
Thyme, dry 40 g
Turmeric 100 g
*Zereshk 25g

Ground spices
*Cassia bark 25 g
Chilli powder 100 g
Cinnamon 25 g
*Clove 25 g
Cummin, white 100 g
*Garlic powder 100 g
*Ginger powder 100 g
Paprika 100 g
Pepper, black 100 g

Pepper, white 100 g
*Sumak 65g
Turmeric 100 g

Spice mixtures
Aromatic salt 100 g
Baharat 20 g
*Curry powder, mild 20 g
Gormeh sabzi 2 oz
Kookoo sabzi 2 oz
*La kama 20 g
Lebanese mixture 20 g
*Ras-el-hanout 30 g
*Za'atar 65 g
*Zhug 25 g

Nuts
Almonds, ground
Almonds, whole
Hazelnuts
Pine nuts 100 g
Pistachio 50 g
Walnut

Dry foods
*Apricot
Chickpeas 500 g
Couscous 500 g
Fava (ful medames) beans 500 g
Ful nabed (broad beans) 500 g
*Loomi (lime) 2 oz
Masoor dhal 500 g
*Melokhia (Egyptian leaves) 2 oz
Sultanas

Flours
Chapatti, brown 500 g

Cornflour
Plain, white (all-purpose)
Strong white
Wholemeal

Oils
Hazelnut
Olive
Sesame
Soya
Sunflower
Vegetable
Walnut
Smen (ghee) 200 g

Canned foods
Chickpeas 14 oz
Fava (ful medames) beans 14 oz
Harissa hot sauce 140 g
*Haricot white beans

Other items
Filo pastry
Lemon juice, bottled
*Milk powder
Orange-blossom water 50 ml
*Red food colouring, dry 25 g
Rice, basmati 2 kg
Rose water 50 ml
Sea salt
Sesame paste (tahine) 100 g
*Vine leaves
Wheat, cracked (burghul) 500 g
*Wheat, whole

INDEX